# How to Create a 'No-Complaining' Organizational Culture

## (…And Why It Will Be Good for Everyone)

SCOTT R. MAURER

Remedium Publications
Alexandria, VA


Cover Design: vikncharlie

ISBN-13: 978-1-7346264-0-7

Author Website: www.remediumsolutions.com

# Note to the Reader

I did not design this book primarily to be read and set aside, but rather to be used as a practical reference by everyone in your organization. I've tried to pack a lot of information into a relatively small space. Therefore, I have avoided using an overabundance of anecdotes and stories in favor of occasional brief examples that I think will embody the concept I am trying to convey and allow the reader to move on quickly.

For this same reason, I've decided not to include footnotes. While I do refer to "research" to reinforce certain points, I did not think the average reader of this book would have an interest in cited academic studies. Those who are can find a list of references at my firm's website: www.remediumsolutions.com.

Readers with advanced management training might come across ideas with they are already familiar. But CEOs and other executives should bear in mind that many, if not most, people in their organizations will *not* be familiar with the concepts in this book, no matter how elementary. Executives can use the ideas in the book as a simple paradigm they can employ to promote a healthy workplace culture. My intention is that the skills and framework found in the book will facilitate the more complex initiatives and messages executives would like to convey to their employees.

The book can be used as a sort of agreement to which everyone in the organization can refer to effect positive cultural change. I have included questions for reflection and discussion after each chapter, and I encourage teammates to go through some of them together. I recommend that you read with a pen in hand to take notes for future reference. I have deliberately left room in the text for note taking. Small sticky tabs can also be helpful to mark pages you are likely to revisit repeatedly.

My hope is that you will find this book helpful and practical. I wrote it to assist you in creating real, positive, enduring organizational transformation. If you have questions about any part of the book, I always encourage readers to contact me. I will do my best to respond promptly. You can reach me at **scott@remediumsolutions.com**.

# CONTENTS

## SOLUTION ONE
## A CULTURE OF HONORING HONESTY

## SOLUTION TWO
## A CULTURE OF PROBLEM NAMING AND
## PROBLEM SOLVING

## SOLUTION THREE
## A CULTURE OF SELF-REFLECTION AND SUPPORT

## APPENDICES

CHAPTER ONE

# A 'No Complaining' Culture

With a title like "how to create a 'no complaining' organizational culture," the first thing I should do is explain what I am *not* saying.

Let me assure you that I'm not suggesting employees adopt a posture of blind acceptance towards their workplace fate, no matter how bad things get. I'm not suggesting that organizations adopt some sort of gulag mentality of peer pressure that coerces employees to remain silent under threat of being reported to the authorities. I'm not trying to give dictatorial leaders a weapon to silence those who languish under their yoke.

What I am saying is that complaining, properly defined, hurts everybody. It infects co-workers. It turns off customers. It discourages leaders. It even wounds the one doing the complaining!

The solution, however, is not to simply stamp out complaining. Complaining doesn't just go away. It shows up again in some other place in some other form. No, the solution is to transform complaining from something destructive into something constructive. Transforming complaining in this way makes the organization a more enjoyable place to work, more efficient, and more effective. When this happens, everyone benefits.

# Healthy Organizational Culture (the Real Goal)

Before we continue the discussion about complaining, I should come clean and confess that eliminating complaining is not my ultimate goal. What I really want to help you achieve is the creation of a healthy organizational culture. Complaining, as we'll see, is simply an instrument we will use to get there.

When I use the term "culture," I'm not referring to whether the organization wears suits or jeans, or whether it is committed to innovation, social action, or some other broad theme. These things will vary with different organizations. Rather, I'm talking about a culture that naturally heals, nurtures, and enhances the relational and emotional health of its people. That doesn't sound very sexy but bear with me for a moment because it is key to everything else you want to do.

Relational health refers to how people in the workplace *relate to one another*. We might also just call this "teamwork" in its most general sense. Emotional health refers to the wellbeing of each *individual* in the organization. There is an important relationship between emotional and relational health. When individual health is bad, it can affect relational heath—that is, relationships with other people. Likewise, when relational health is bad, it affects the emotional (and sometimes physical) health of the individuals on the team.

Marcus Buckingham and Ashley Goodall, in their book *Nine Lies about Work*, found that people care less about the organization they work for and more about the teams they are on. Specifically, people care more about the relationships they have with their immediate leaders, followers, and team members. The point is that the organization's big cultural themes (which is where most organizations focus) matter less than the sub-cultures of each of the teams that make up the organization (which Buckingham and Goodall say most organizations ignore).

When I talk about creating culture, therefore, I am not referring to the typical things people mean when they emphasize organizational culture—like shared vision, a common mission, brand promotion, wearing company T-shirts, or anything else aimed at engendering this high-level organizational culture. I am referring to something less sensational but far more important—a culture that naturally works to correct, preserve, and develop the relational and emotional health of everyone in the organization.

This will look different in different organizations because certainly, every organization has a different feel (something we often call "culture"). But a 'no complaining' culture is one that naturally tends the relational and emotional health of everyone in the organization. When this is happening, all of the other things that most organizations value (e.g., productivity, innovation, quality, employee retention and recruitment, etc.) fall into place. When this is not happening, however, talk about organizational culture, values, goals, and mission are not much more than window dressing.

# What is Complaining?

I mentioned that complaining will be the instrument we use to create a healthy organizational culture. So, as we begin to think about transforming complaining, let me give you my definition of complaining:

**Complaining is a verbal or physical expression of concern or frustration that is destructive (as opposed to constructive) in nature.**

That's pretty straight forward, but let's break it apart a little.

The most obvious type of complaining most of us think about is the verbal expression kind. This is expressing concern or frustration with our mouths, saying something like, "it's so hot in here" or "I can't believe the boss made that decision" or "these employees have no work ethic."

But we can also express concern or frustration with our bodies, like rolling our eyes or shaking our heads. Furthermore, complaining can take the form of things we do (acts of commission) or things we deliberately don't do (acts of omission). For example, an act of omission might be refusing to come to an all hands meeting because "it's just going to be more of the same nonsense, and I'm sick of hearing it." An act of commission might be something like deliberately sabotaging a project deadline.

Complaining is also destructive, not constructive. That is, complaining tears down rather than builds up. It aims to harm rather than heal. It has no productive merit or value. This is a critical point to remember when seeking to transform complaining into something beneficial. When a verbal or physical expression of concern or frustration becomes truly constructive, it is no longer complaining. It becomes something else—something positive, welcome, and important.

## What Is the Problem and Why Does It Matter?

I am not saying that complaining is always wrong. Several years ago, roughly 20,000 Google employees walked out of work to protest their concern about sexual harassment in the workplace. According to my definition, these employees were definitely complaining—and complaining vociferously! They expressed their concern verbally and physically. And this walkout was destructive because it incinerated thousands of hours of highly paid tech workers' labor.

But was it wrong? I would argue that it was right and even necessary. As I understand it, some positive changes were made as a consequence. Nevertheless, a better solution would have been to resolve the Google employees' concerns in more constructive ways. The reason they had to complain is that they weren't getting resolution any other way. The result was destruction. (Of course, the harassment perpetrated against some of these Google women was destructive also, but I am trying to bring clarity to my working definition of complaining since it will be important to the rest of the book.)

The Google example illustrates a very large-scale complaint. But complaining (i.e., "verbal or physical expressions of concern or frustration that are destructive in nature") is happening on a smaller scale every day in most organizations. This is a tragedy when one considers the destruction that complaining causes.

**Complaining destroys people**. It destroys the complainer and those around her—friends, family, co-workers, customers.

**Complaining destroys organizations.** It destroys products, services, ideas, and innovations that might have contributed something good to the world but have instead become rubble piles.

If given a choice, would you rather be someone who builds, creates, and constructs? Or, someone who destroys?

Certainly, we can think of things that are fun to destroy. When I was renovating my kitchen, my kids and I had a great time tearing down a wall with a sledgehammer. But even then, we had an eye toward the construction of a new room in which our family could cook and eat together.

When the forest service executes a controlled burn in a section of woodland, the purpose is not ultimately destruction. Most of us would register that as a tragic waste. Rather, the destruction of the old trees makes room for healthy new growth. In other words, the aim was never destruction, but creation.

So, would you rather be a creator or a destroyer? Most of us would choose to be creators. But that means that we must know how to construct rather than destroy. When it comes to organizational culture, therefore, we need to learn how to transform destructive complaining into something constructive.

When the entire organization is committed to creation, not destruction, it becomes far easier for individual employees to stop complaining and start being constructive. If the organization is unwilling to do this, people feel they have little choice but to complain—whether on a small scale by talking behind the boss's back or on a large scale as it happened at Google.

So how do organizations transform complaining from something destructive into something constructive?

## Learning to See Complaining as a Symptom

An important start to transforming complaining from something destructive into something constructive is learning to see complaining as a helpful symptom that points to something in the organization that needs to be addressed. In that sense, *complaining is an opportunity* because it's even worse when there are festering problems you don't know about that manifest themselves only when they explode.

Understanding complaining as a symptom of a problem that needs to be addressed rather than the problem to be eliminated is key to creating a no complaining culture. When we understand complaining as a symptom, we take the time to go after the problem rather than merely modifying the complaining behavior.

If our primary focus is eliminating complaining behavior, we will concentrate on the wrong things. We will be tempted to resort to whatever coercion we can muster to silence the complainers. This could be overt like threatening punishment for employees who complain. But that would be draconian, and I doubt many organizations could get away with that.

What is more likely is something more subtle. For example, those who complain could be labeled as troublemakers. Everyone knows that being branded with such a label will hurt your credibility and opportunity for advancement. I have even seen this come in the form of something more righteous sounding, like an organization claiming to have a value of not talking negatively because "we have a positive culture." Having a positive culture is great, but when positivity becomes a façade that everyone is expected to put up, the organization risks silencing people.

Remember, I am not encouraging complaining. This book is about creating a 'no-complaining' culture. But we don't accomplish that through silencing people by modifying their behavior. The problems causing the complaining don't go away. They go underground. In fact, if I had to choose between a complaining culture and a silenced culture, I would choose a complaining culture any day. At least I would have more opportunity to understand some of the problems that exist in my organization.

Rather, the way to create a no complaining culture is to recognize complaining as a potentially helpful indicator telling us we have an opportunity to address a problem and providing a map to its root. Once there, we can engage the issue productively. When this is done well, destructive complaining begins to change into constructive creation.

So 'no complaining' does not mean "be quiet and take it." It means solve the problem constructively. When this happens, the organization will thrive, and the people will be happier. We're not shutting down complaining, we're transforming it! How to do that is what this book aims to describe.

## An Important Note for Organizational Leaders

If you are an organizational leader, I'd like to make an important point before we move forward.

I am a realist when it comes to transformation. I don't want to just write some thoughts that people read and forget. I want to see real beneficial change happen in your organization. So, let me make an appeal to you as you consider the contents of this book.

I once heard Brene Brown talk about her leap into Internet fame. If you're not familiar with her, she is a psychological researcher who focuses on shame and vulnerability. Some years ago, she gave a TED Talk that catapulted her into the spotlight. Almost overnight, she had become a YouTube celebrity because she spoke about something that deeply resonated with people all over the world – namely shame and vulnerability.

Brene said that she soon began to receive calls from business leaders asking her to come speak to their employees. Here is what I found interesting and revealing. Most of these business leaders asked her not to speak about shame and vulnerability (her areas of research focus). Rather, they asked her to talk about innovation, creativity, and change. This is telling.

It's not that innovation, creativity, and change are unreasonable things for leaders to desire from their people. They are very reasonable. Innovation and creativity are things that help people come up with new products, services, and ways of doing things that make money and advance mission. An ability to embrace change helps organizations weather market fluctuations and the developments that innovation and creativity bring. But notice that innovation, creativity, and change are things that *employers need* from employees.

Now consider shame and vulnerability. These are the topics that made Brene Brown's TED Talk one of the most viewed ever. Why? Because they resonated so strongly with the deepest needs of people all over the world. Yet, when business leaders asked Brene to speak to their employees, they asked her not to speak about shame and vulnerability, which is *what the employees needed*. They asked her to speak on innovation, creativity, and change, which is what they (the leaders) needed.

You might say, "well, I pay those employees, and I would be paying Brene Brown to speak to them, so why shouldn't I have her speak about what I need from those employees?" I want to suggest that it doesn't work this way. To put it crassly, this is like employers saying to their employees, "just shut up and be innovative, creative, and changeable."

The reason so many people resonated with Brene's discussion of shame and vulnerability is that they know there are things about them that are broken and wounded. I have coached and counseled hundreds of people for thousands of hours, and I can tell you that even those people most of us would consider successful and together have areas of weakness they do everything they can to keep hidden. They hide these places from others, and sometimes they hide them from themselves. So, when someone like Brene Brown calls out areas of weakness like shame and vulnerability, people feel a sense of relief that they are not alone and a sense of hope that they can experience some healing.

So what is my point? I'm saying that the things leaders want (i.e., innovation, creativity, and change) are stifled by the brokenness their people experience. Thus, the way to stimulate innovation, creativity, and change is by first addressing the brokenness. And yet these business leaders completely missed this and asked Brene Brown to ignore the things their employees needed and move straight to the things they needed from their employees.

Let me give you an illustration that I hope will clarify this important point. If someone wants to have a nice lawn, many people will spend a lot of money on grass seed and fertilizer. This sounds reasonable, right? The problem is that if the soil is not well prepared, the grass seed and fertilizer will wash away with the first heavy rain. Not only will the grass not grow, but a lot of money will have been wasted.

Knowing this, consider a scenario where a gardener comes along and tells the homeowner that he should first *prepare* the soil. Otherwise, the grass seed won't grow, and he'll waste his money. Nevertheless, the homeowner orders the gardener to skip the soil preparation, lay down the grass seed, and "just make it grow!" Well, of course, we would recognize the homeowner's folly.

Yet, it's the same with organizations. If your organizational soil is not well prepared, you can spend a lot of money on initiatives designed to foster innovation, stimulate creativity, and facilitate change. But much of it will wash away if the emotional and relational health of your people is poor.

In this book, I will be providing ways to prepare the organizational soil *as well as* lay the grass seed and fertilizer. My goal is to help your organization transform destructive complaining into constructive creation. I want this approach to work for you, so I'm calling your attention to the proclivities of many business leaders like the ones who wanted Brene Brown to skip the soil preparation and "just make the grass grow." You might be tempted to do this. If you are, you'd be like many other business leaders, so I'm not being critical. I just want your grass seed to grow, not wash away. Therefore, I'm trying to help you avoid this mistake.

With that said, I'll explain how to use this book.

# How to Use This Book

This book should be used as a sort of agreement between all the people in your organization. This means everyone, from the executives to the line. Having a set of principles that are common to all involved will increase the likelihood that those principles will be effective.

If only one person learns something and puts it into practice, there is less chance that it will work. In marriage counseling, for example, sometimes one spouse refuses to participate in the process. That makes it extremely difficult to help because one spouse is trying to practice techniques that the other doesn't recognize or know how to engage. It's a whole different process when you can work with both spouses at the same time. In this case, they have both bought into the technique. Now, when one spouse practices a technique that they both agreed to practice, the other spouse knows how to interact with that technique productively.

If everyone buys into the techniques mentioned in this book, it is far more likely that people will recognize it when others put them into practice, and this will facilitate productive reciprocal engagement. To make this easier, I have included exercises and discussion questions where I think they will be helpful.

Don't worry, I'm not going to ask you to pass around a talking stick, stand in a circle in the middle of the room, or play musical chairs. I think it's far better to treat adults like adults. The principles and techniques in this book are designed to work with a variety of personality types and to guide people within the natural flow of human interaction. In other words, I want this to ultimately feel practical, natural, and effective (even though some things may feel a little awkward at first). When this is done well, it facilitates all the other goals and initiatives people want to pursue in their organizations.

Finally, I strongly recommend that you do not skip any parts of the book. Every element is there for a reason (recall the analogy of preparing the soil before laying the grass seed and fertilizer). To give you a sense of the importance of each section, here is a summary of the chapters.

**Chapter 1: A 'No Complaining' Culture**—this first chapter establishes the book's real goal of healthy cultural change and defines complaining and how it can be used to transform culture.

**Chapter 2: Why a 'No Complaining' Culture Matters**—Changing organizational culture takes work and commitment, so we'll discuss the benefits of putting in the effort and the consequences of ignoring complaining.

**Chapter 3: Why People Complain**—To understand the best way to address complaining, we must understand the reasons people complain. We'll discuss four main reasons: people feel helpless; people are frustrated by a problem; people are in pain; people have a bad attitude.

**Chapter 4: The Solution**—Now that we've understood the four main reasons people complain, we can identify the solution for each of those reasons.

**SOLUTION ONE: A Culture of Honoring Honesty**—the solution to people feeling helpless is to create a culture on honoring honesty. Chapters Five, Six, and Seven describe how to accomplish this.

**Chapter 5: Learn Productive Interpersonal Communication**—people must work together to be effective, and this means they must communicate well. We'll discuss some important ground rules people can use to improve interpersonal communications. That will help everyone feel more empowered and heard.

**Chapter 6: Cultivate Vertical Respect**—there are some unique communication dynamics between leaders and followers. Each must understand these dynamics in order to really hear and understand the other.

**Chapter 7: Agree to Use Designated Communications Channels**— Mass communication is difficult, but it's an important way that leaders and followers share ideas and stay informed. We'll discuss ways to make this more efficient.

**SOLUTION TWO: A Culture of Problem Naming and Problem Solving**—the solution to people feeling frustrated by a problem is to create a culture where people naturally act to resolve that problem or learn to accept it. Chapters Eight, Nine, and Ten discuss practical ways to do this.

**Chapter 8: Resolve 'Small Problems' as They Come Up**—small problems are like low hanging fruit. They are opportunities to score tiny victories that add up. The key is knowing how to move into action.

**Chapter 9: Make a Plan to Resolve Medium Problems**—medium problems are more involved, so people need to know how to approach them as mini-projects and resolve them.

**Chapter 10: Identify and Acknowledge 'Large Problems'**—large problems are not going away any time soon. So, people must learn how to accept and live with them.

**SOLUTION THREE: A Culture of Self-Reflection and Support**— the solution to people being in pain and having a bad attitude is to create a culture of self-reflection and support. Chapters Eleven and Twelve discuss practical ways to accomplish this.

**Chapter 11: Develop Self-Awareness**—the goal of self-reflection is self-awareness. We'll discuss ways in which people can become more aware of their motivations and behaviors (especially those that are difficult to see) and grow into everything they can be.

**Chapter 12: Establish Peer Support**—people bring their problems to work and bring their work frustrations home. A healthy peer support structure can help employees become more resilient and develop as people. It can also create meaning and purpose for peer supporters.

**Chapter 13: Creating a "No Complaining" Organizational Culture**—in this final chapter, we'll discuss some practical next steps you can take to pursue a 'no complaining' organizational culture.

**Appendices A-G**—in these appendices, I've included some documents and templates that can assist you with creating a 'no complaining' organizational culture.

# Questions for Reflection and Discussion

1. What do you think of the definition of complaining as: "a verbal or physical expression of concern or frustration that is destructive (as opposed to constructive) in nature"?

2. Have you ever thought of complaining as something destructive?

3. If given a choice, would you rather be someone who builds, creates, and constructs? Or, someone who destroys?

4. Have you ever thought about complaining as a symptom that can help point you to a problem that you then have an opportunity to address?

5. What do you think about the illustration of laying grass seed and fertilizer without first preparing the soil? Can you think of some examples of how organizations do this?

CHAPTER TWO

# Why a 'No-Complaining' Culture Matters

Change management guru John Kotter emphasizes that people will not embrace change until they have a sense of urgency about why change is necessary. With that in mind, let me encourage you not to skip this section. It's important to develop a sense of urgency about why creating a 'no complaining' organizational culture matters.

To get into this section then, let's review my working definition of complaining:

**Complaining is a verbal or physical expression of concern or frustration that is destructive (as opposed to constructive) in nature.**

Anything destructive is going to cause damage (by definition!). In this chapter, I will try to make the case that complaining damages the complainer, co-workers, leaders, and the organization as a whole. Let's take them one at a time.

# Complaining Hurts Complainers

In one sense, complaining feels good. When we do it, it can feel like a natural release—it just comes out of us. But this is deceptive because complaining poisons our soul. Let's look at brain science to better understand how this "poisoning of our soul" happens.

We might say that complaining literally "rewires" your brain. Remember, I'm talking about something destructive—with no purpose. I don't mean constructively talking through something that concerns or hurts you (which I'll explain further in Chapters Eleven and Twelve).

There is something called brain neuroplasticity. It basically means that your brain's "wiring" can and does change. When I talk about a brain's "wiring," I'm referring to the way that the brain's cells function and interact, and the way the chemicals and electrical impulses in the brain behave. This gets complex, so we'll just call it "wiring." The idea of neuroplasticity is that your brain wiring is not entirely fixed—it can change. That can be good news and bad news, depending upon *how* your brain's wiring changes.

The part of neuroplasticity that is important to this discussion is the idea that your brain's wiring changes based upon certain things that affect it. At the same time, the wiring in your brain affects the way your brain processes things. It's is a little bit of a chicken-and-the-egg sort of concept.

For example, if your brain is wired to notice and dwell on negative things, you will tend to notice and dwell on negative things. You'll notice that the room is too hot, that your co-worker's music is too loud, that the project you're working on is going to take a lot of time to complete, that your boss is grumpy, and so on. You'll also tend to dwell and obsess about these things such that they start to affect your mood and effectiveness.

On the other hand, if a negative thing is happening around you (like a hot room, distracting music, challenging deadlines, or a grumpy boss), it will potentially have an impact on your brain's wiring. Specifically, it can rewire your brain to be more sensitive to the negative thing that is happening around you.

Here is where this matters to our discussion about complaining. Our thoughts can affect our brain's wiring *as if* the thing we are thinking about is actually happening. So, if my boss walks by with a scowl on his face and doesn't say hello, I might notice that he's in a bad mood. But let's say I then begin to *re-imagine* the look on his face and start thinking about how he should be more inspiring and positive. Maybe I envision him yelling at me about whatever is bothering him. As I'm dwelling on this, I start getting irritated, tense, and distracted.

What's happening here is that the stuff going on in my imagination is having the same effect *as if* it were actually happening right in front of me. In other words, the brief interaction with my boss impacted me a little bit, but every moment I spend replaying and amplifying the incident in my mind affects me even more!

But it gets even more interesting. There is emerging evidence revealing that complaining to another person makes this effect even worse. The research suggests that complaining with no constructive goal (e.g., solving the problem or learning to accept the thing you are tempted to complain about) rewires our brains to be more sensitive and irritated by the thing that we are complaining about. Therefore, after my boss walks by without saying hello, if I then lean over to my co-worker and complain that the boss is grumpy, my brain can become even more wired to complain.

Having a brain that is wired to complain is not healthy for you. Complaining impacts your emotional and physical health, and it is associated with higher incidents of depression and anxiety. It also causes increases in stress and the many negative consequences associated with stress, like cardiovascular disease, immune system suppression, and decreased cognitive functioning.

The good news is that thinking positively, practicing gratitude, and constructively engaging problems can rewire your brain in healthy ways. Remember, brain neuroplasticity can work both ways. I'm not talking about ignoring problems or faking positivity. Rather, I mean that if you can reduce your complaining, your brain can become re-wired so that you naturally tend to complain less. In other words, not complaining can become easier. We'll discuss how you can do that in Chapter Eleven.

For now, let me sum this all up. When you complain (as I've defined complaining), your brain's wiring changes and becomes more sensitive to the very things you are complaining about. Your brain also becomes inclined to complain even more. And brains wired for a tendency to complain have a negative impact on emotional and physical health. In other words, complaining harms the complainer.

## Complaining Hurts Teams

The well-known leadership coach Marshall Goldsmith surveyed 200 of his coaching clients to determine how much time they spent complaining. He found that most of his clients said they complained between 10-20 hours per month. This was consistent with the figures he had read in similar studies. That's a lot of money and time wasted annually on complaining. In an organization of 100 people with an average salary of $50,000/year wasting 10 hours/month complaining, that's about $300,000 wasted each year.

But it's more than just time-wasting. Complaining is contagious. Research suggests that people tend to appropriate the thoughts of the people they are around and that the most common response to a complainer is to agree with the complaint. In the previous section, we saw how complaining hurts the complainer. This research shows that at least two people are suffering the damage done by complaining, since the complainer and the person being complained to are both in agreement with the complaint. And if there are more people involved in the complaining session, there's a good chance that even more people are being harmed by the original complainer.

Imagine that some of the people involved in that complaining session go to other people and complain. Now you start to see a multiplication effect. More and more people in the organization having their brains re-wired for a natural propensity to complain—not to mention the damage it's doing their emotional and physical health.

There are other ways complaining damages teams. Scholars who study complaining make a distinction between "instrumental" and "non-instrumental" complaining. Instrumental complaining is when a person points out something that needs to be corrected to positively affect change. It is what I am calling constructive engagement. I wouldn't call it complaining at all, especially if it's done well (which we'll discuss in Chapters Eleven and Twelve). Non-instrumental complaining, on the other hand, is precisely what I *am* calling complaining. It serves no constructive purpose. It is complaining for the sake of complaining. It is destructive.

The research suggests that most people engage in non-instrumental complaining. In a team setting, this means they are not solving problems that need to be solved. All teams encounter hurdles as they pursue their mission. They must be able to get over these hurdles, or they will become paralyzed. If most of the complaining they do is unproductive and purposeless, the team is not developing the problem-solving skills it needs to be effective.

Furthermore, this non-instrumental complaining is frequently about another person—perhaps another person on the team. When this is the case, it likely indicates that the team doesn't have the ability to deal with others who they perceive as difficult. The trouble with this is that teams are made up of people, and they must work with people on other teams. People can misunderstand each other, ignore each other, and sometimes they just don't get along very well. Nevertheless, effective teams learn to overcome these interpersonal challenges. When team members are engaging in non-instrumental complaining about other people, it is a sure sign that they do not know how to overcome these interpersonal barriers.

The solution is for teams to stop complaining, learn how to engage in constructive problem solving, and develop the conflict resolution skills that will enhance (not destroy) human relationships. Developing these skills will make the team more effective in every way. Conversely, unchecked complaining will destroy the team dynamic, allow the team to complain about problems rather than resolve them, and poison the souls of the team members.

Complaining hurts teams.

## Complaining Demoralizes Leaders

Since we often perceive leaders as having some sort of power over us, it is easy for us to forget that leaders are subject to the same emotions as anyone in the organization. Another way to say this is that it's easy to forget that leaders are human too. That means they can become demoralized like anyone. Only true sociopaths don't care what others think. While there are plenty of leaders out there who could develop their leadership abilities, few are true sociopaths. Whether they show it or not, it matters to them what people think about them and the organizations they lead. When complaining abounds, leaders can easily become demoralized.

The human side to this is simply that we should respect leaders just as we should respect anyone else in the organization. It's certainly true that nobody in an organization is more valuable than any other person. The chief executive of an organization is no more valuable than a first-year intern working for free or the people who empty the trash at the end of the day. Nevertheless, we can't forget that those in leadership have feelings, families, friends, and flaws—as do all of us. Just as we expect leaders to show us understanding and grace, we should offer leaders the same courtesy. It's the right thing to do.

But there is a practical side to this. When leaders are demoralized, it is bad for the organization. While leaders are no more valuable than anyone else, they do often have a disproportionate impact on the organization—for better or for worse. Therefore, it is in everyone's best interest that leaders feel good about their role, the organization, and the people they lead.

Leaders tend to set the tone for the organizations they lead (whether it's the entire organization or just a working group). When leaders are excited, it can be contagious. When they dread coming to work every day, you can bet this will have a deflating effect on everyone who works for them. When leaders are demoralized because of complaining, they will be less inclined to take risks or make changes that could benefit the organization. They will tend to isolate themselves when they should be wading in to help resolve the problems giving rise to the complaining. They will begin to see those they lead as their adversaries, rather than as their responsibilities.

Also, one of the jobs of a leader is to coordinate those they lead. When leaders do this well, the employees in the organization can be more effective. If people are complaining about a leader, however, they are probably not paying much attention to the leader's coordination efforts. Therefore, these complainers will tend to become frustrated as they realize that their efforts are being duplicated, stifled, or unreciprocated by others in the organization who *are* doing their best to operate in harmony with the leader's coordination efforts.

I do want to make something clear about this point. Employees can and should still be able to express their concerns about a leader or disagree with that leader. My warnings here regarding the effect of complaining on leaders is not to suggest that people give leaders a free pass or never raise concerns. That would be unhealthy for everyone— including the leader. But everyone in the organization should learn to do this constructively, skillfully, and respectfully, not in destructive ways that qualify as complaining (we'll discuss some specific ways to do this in Chapters Five and Six). Leadership is challenging enough, and complaining demoralizes leaders.

## Complaining Indicates Disengaged Employees

If there is a lot of complaining happening in the workplace, it likely indicates the presence of disengaged employees. Disengaged employees are apathetic or even hostile toward the organization. There has been a lot of research conducted about employee engagement over the last 20 years by major business research firms such as Gallup, Gartner, and Forrester, and by elite business schools, such as Harvard Business School. This research is revealing a much deeper understanding of what constitutes an engaged or disengaged employee, the factors that contribute to employee engagement and disengagement, and the effect of engaged and disengaged workers on the organization.

The research shows that organizations with high levels of employee engagement significantly outperform those with low employee engagement. For example, the Enterprise Engagement Alliance publishes the "Engaged Company Stock Index." This index tracks the long-term stock market value of 47 companies with high levels of customer, employee, and community engagement. It is interesting to note that the Engaged Company Stock Index has outperformed the S&P 500 (including dividends) by 37.1 percentage points since October 1, 2012.

On the other hand, research also shows that disengaged employees have a significant negative impact on organizations. For example, quality errors in low engagement organizations are considerably higher than those with high engagement. Disengaged employees tend to provide substantially poorer customer service than their highly engaged counterparts. It is more difficult to recruit and retain employees in organizations with a high proportion of disengaged employees. And disengaged employees are much less productive than highly engaged employees.

Because the data overwhelmingly demonstrates the importance of employees, investors are beginning to place more value on human capital. Accounting and valuation metrics have traditionally looked at employees as an expense, but there is increasing momentum to regard employees as a capital investment. Valuation is moving away from traditional price/earnings metrics to include other elements of a firm's health. In November 2019, the Harvard Law School Forum on Corporate Governance and Financial Regulation released a statement entitled, "How and Why Human Capital Disclosures are Evolving." An excerpt from the statement reads:

A company's intangible assets, which include human capital and culture, are now estimated to comprise on average 52% of a company's market value ... In this era of disruption, talent and culture have leapt to the forefront of thinking around enabling strategy and innovation and creating long-term value. Accordingly, human capital has rapidly emerged as a critical focus area for stakeholders. There is a clear and growing market appetite to understand how companies are managing and measuring human capital.

Larry Fink, Chairman and CEO of investment giant BlackRock, recently wrote to CEOs around the world, reminding them that investments in people will be increasingly vital to the maximization of long-term value creation. SEC Chair Jay Clayton is making overtures about possible regulatory requirements around the reporting of human capital investment and procedures. The Davos Conference recently updated its manifesto to emphasize the importance of businesses engaging all stakeholders, including employees. The Business Roundtable has made similar statements.

To facilitate this building momentum, the International Organization for Standardization (ISO) has released (or is in the process of developing) the following standards related to human capital:

- ISO 10018 Quality People Management
- ISO 30414 Human Capital Management
- ISO 30409 Knowledge Management
- ISO 30401 Recruitment
- ISO 10267 Assessment Services

All of this means that the handwriting is on the wall. For organizations to continue to compete in the marketplace, they will need to pay increasing attention to their organizational health. That will include efforts to assess and optimize employee engagement. Complaining erodes employee engagement and is an indication of employee disengagement. The process of creating a 'no complaining' organizational culture, on the other hand, will significantly increase employee engagement and overall organizational health.

So, let's begin to consider *how* to create a 'no complaining' organizational culture.

## Questions for Reflection and Discussion

1. How does complaining hurt those doing the complaining? Were you aware of this?

2. How does complaining hurt teams? Have you ever noticed this happening? Can you give an example?

3. How does complaining demoralize leaders? Have you ever experienced this as a leader? Were you aware that your leader might experience this?

4. What is a disengaged employee? Why might complaining indicate the presence of disengaged employees? Why does this matter?

5. After reading this chapter, how important do you think it is to address complaining? Why?

CHAPTER THREE

# Why People Complain

To be able to fix a problem, it helps to understand it. Since we're trying to create a 'no complaining' organizational culture, let's dig into the reasons people complain.

Imagine you have a horse that won't run. You think the horse is just stubborn or untrainable. But, if the reason the horse won't run is that it has a stone in its hoof, you can kick it all day, but it will still not run because you're attacking the wrong problem. If, on the other hand, you make some careful diagnosis and find the stone in the horse's hoof, you have an opportunity to solve the real problem. If you remove the stone, it is much more likely that the horse will run when you kick.

The same principle applies to complaining. Why do people complain? There are several reasons. Each has a different solution, so it's important to understand the *cause* of the complaining. That will make it easier to apply the solution that will be most effective.

First, let's review (again!) the definition of complaining that we're working with:

*Complaining is* a verbal or physical expression of concern or frustration that is destructive (as opposed to constructive) in nature.

In my observations, people complain for at least four general reasons:

- They feel helpless
- They are frustrated by a problem
- They are in pain
- They have a bad attitude

Research suggests that most people complain about a person when they complain, but I did not include "people" in my list of possible reasons for complaining. That's because the complaint about the person could be for any of the reasons that I did list. For example, a person may be behaving in ways that the complainer doesn't feel she can do anything about (feeling helpless). A person might be a project gatekeeper who is impeding the complainer's progress (frustrated by a problem). A person might be treating the complainer in hurtful ways (causing pain). Or, a person might be difficult for the complainer to work with (bad attitude).

To better understand, let's take a closer look at each of these reasons that people complain.

# Feeling Helpless

One of the main reasons people complain is that they feel helpless.

I've spent many hours helping people work out their conflicts with one another. This could be spouses, parents and children, co-workers, leaders and followers—you get the picture. Usually, one of the parties involved is convinced that the way to resolve the conflict is for the other party to change his or her behavior. That could mean start doing something, stop doing something, or do something differently. Often one of the people involved is displaying behavior that seems excessive. Understandably, the other person is confused and unhappy about this behavior and wants to focus all mediation effort upon it. In other words, the one person *complains* about the other's excessive behavior.

Frequently, the one displaying the excessive behavior is doing so because he or she feels helpless. The person might not even be aware of that feeling of helplessness. But the excessive behavior is a move of desperation borne out of a feeling of powerlessness against whatever the other person is doing that feels so hurtful or threatening. By the way, it's likely that the person behaving excessively has also been complaining to someone else about whatever the other person has been doing that the one with the excessive behavior feels helpless against. Thus, both parties are complaining.

Sometimes it's easiest to grasp an idea with a tangible example. So, let's look at a scenario involving a guy named Jim, who is behaving excessively and complaining *because* he feels helpless.

Jim's boss, Jane, invites him to a meeting. Everyone attending the meeting has a vigorous and productive discussion—except Jim. He sits there with his arms crossed and a scowl on his face, refusing to say anything. Jane notices Jim's passive-aggressive behavior because Jim is making it really obvious! Trying to draw him out, she asks him if he'd like to contribute anything to the discussion. Jim tightens his arms, gives a cynical smile, and says, "nope!" Jane follows up with Jim afterward and asks him why he didn't say anything in the meeting. Jim just says, "I had nothing to contribute." Meanwhile, Jim goes to lunch with his co-worker Stan and complains that Jane is "just like all of them—not interested in anyone's ideas."

Our first instinct might be to say that Jim should be disciplined in some way for acting as he did. That would not be unreasonable based solely on his behavior. But there several things that might explain the behavior. Depending upon what's causing it, discipline might not be the best or most effective option. It might even be counterproductive if it caused the employee to engage in even worse behavior, quit, or get fired. Any of those options would be costly to the organization.

For this case, let's assume that the reason for Jim's behavior is that he feels helpless. Let me explain this further. Jim has been working for the organization for almost a year. He was hired to work for Andrew, who led a department that handled a subject that really interested Jim.

After a week of onboarding, Jim was feeling great about rolling up his sleeves and getting to work. On the last day of the onboarding week, Meg from HR asked to meet with him. She told him that Andrew's department had been reorganized into two departments, one led by Andrew and the other led by Tony. Jim would now be working for Tony. Jim told Meg he had very much wanted to work for Andrew, but she said these decisions are made way above her pay grade. Jim went to see Meg's boss, who told him that once these decisions are made, there is nothing to be done.

Jim decided to hunker down and try to make the best of working for Tony. On his first day, Tony held one-on-one meetings with each of his new staff. Tony sat Jim down and told him what he expected and what Jim would be doing. Jim was crushed. This was nothing like what Andrew had hired him to do. Jim started to explain to Tony that he had a lot of ideas that could benefit the company. He said that Andrew had been excited about them.

Less than a minute into Jim's pitch, Tony held out his hand and said, "let me stop you right there. I'm not Andrew, and that's not what I need from you. Why don't you pull out something to write on, and I'll tell you what I'm going to need you to do." Jim couldn't believe it. Tony didn't even want to hear his ideas. He had been working on them for weeks preparing to start this job. He had gone back to school to become good at this stuff. He felt discouraged.

Three weeks later, Tony's boss, Mary, called an all-hands meeting. Jim had never met Mary—he wasn't sure why. At the meeting, Mary announced that Tony had left the company and Jane was taking his place. Jim didn't feel much one way or another. He was relieved that Tony was gone, but he didn't know anything about Jane. As he drove home that night, he chided himself for feeling so discouraged about the company. "Things happen," he told himself. "Tony was just a bad boss, and everyone gets a bad boss from time to time. I really should give Jane a chance." The more he thought about it, the more encouraged he became. Maybe Jane would be the kind of person who would at least listen to his ideas. He felt he had a lot to offer her!

The next day, Jim went into the office early. He dug out some slides he had prepared to show Tony—slides he never got to show him. He went over them, imagining how appreciative Jane would be. Jane finally came into the office around mid-morning. Jim gave her a few minutes to settle in and knocked on her door. She looked up with an exhausted expression and said flatly, "Can I help you?" That wasn't the response Jim was expecting from his new boss, and it rattled him a little. He regained his composure and said, "Hi, I'm Jim. I work for you. I was hoping to tell you about some ideas I've been working on that I think might interest you." The second he said it, he realized how awkward he had sounded.

Jane closed her eyes for a moment and opened them slowly. "I'm sorry Jim—maybe another time." She looked at him as if her eyes were just parked on his, waiting for him to leave. Jim stared for a moment and felt himself nod and turn away. He walked right by his desk and took an early lunch. Two days later, Jim received an email invitation from Jane to the meeting we discussed at the beginning of this section—the one where Jim sat with his arms crossed, refusing to contribute.

So, what's going on?

Well, I'm not trying to insult your intelligence with this story. I'm sure that as you read this, you were astute enough to see all sorts of places that any of the characters could have acted more wisely. But I want to suggest that you and I have the advantage of this omniscient perspective as observers of the story. When we are one of the actors in real life, however, it's usually not so easy. We are much more inclined to be disoriented, caught off guard, and subject to our shortcomings.

I want to suggest that in this case, the main driver of Jim's behavior was his feeling of helplessness. He felt placed in a job for which he had not been hired, with a boss who had no interest in really listening to him. He felt he had no appeal to anyone who could help. His hopes had been repeatedly peaked then dashed in a way that made him feel he was just being tossed around on the waves.

The last straw was when his new boss, Jane, had made it clear that she too was uninterested in anything he had to say. Jim didn't know what to do. Something inside him snapped, and he decided that if nobody cared about who he was and what he thought, he would simply refuse to offer anything. He wanted to shout his frustration all over the office, but he obviously couldn't do that. So instead, he "shouted" with his body language, tone of voice, and terse words in the meeting. And then he complained to his colleague over lunch.

I'm not saying that Jim's perceptions were entirely accurate. We'll see later in the chapter that they were not. Nevertheless, it is how Jim *felt*. And that is what we must deal with if we're going to understand the best way to address this situation.

I've seen it many times. When people act out in some form, they are frequently feeling desperate, helpless, and unheard. They act out because they don't know what else to do. Most commonly, this takes the form of passive-aggressive behavior and complaining to colleagues, as was the case with Jim. Sometimes it manifests in a much larger scale act of complaining, like the Google walkout we discussed in Chapter One. Those people felt helpless—like nobody was listening to their concerns or doing anything about them—so they acted out in a dramatic way. (In Chapters Five, Six, and Seven, we'll discuss some practical ways to communicate effectively, so that people feel empowered and heard.)

Many people who respond out of a sense of helplessness are not aware of their behavior or why they behave as they do. That's why self-awareness becomes so vital (as we'll see in Chapter Eleven). We must consider whether a person is complaining because of a feeling of helplessness. Remember, it doesn't matter if the person really *is* helpless. What's important is whether she *feels* helpless. Certainly, getting a proper perspective on reality might be a part of resolving that feeling of helplessness. But we must first understand the problem in order to address it. So, for now, let's just acknowledge that feeling helpless is a common source of complaining.

## Feeling Frustrated by a Problem

Another reason people complain is that they feel frustrated by a problem. Something in their workflow is getting in their way, slowing them down, keeping them from accomplishing their assignments, and so on. This may be a process, a person, or a circumstance. Consider another example happening on the floor below Jim's.

Barbara has a stack of invoices piling up next to her desk. She is supposed to process the invoices and send them to clients so her firm will get paid. But the pile is getting bigger because Barbara refuses to process more than ten invoices each day. Tom, Barbara's boss, has made it clear that he expects her to process at least 50 invoices each day. The last time Tom spoke to Barbara, he warned her that he was going to write up a formal reprimand if she didn't change. She didn't. The invoices are still piling up, and Tom is contemplating his next move. He complains to his boss Janet that he doesn't know how to get Barbara to be more productive. Meanwhile, Barbara complains to her suitemate Sally that this organization doesn't care about equipping its employees with the tools they need to do their jobs. Sally nods her head in quiet agreement.

Tom is understandably frustrated, as he demonstrates by complaining to Janet. Janet encourages Tom to start formally documenting Barbara's poor performance to pave the way for dismissal if she doesn't improve. That is not unreasonable counsel. The trouble is that Tom's threatening is not seeming to get Barbara to increase her production to acceptable levels. So, what's going on? Is there any way to get Barbara to do what is expected of her? Let's bring in some more information about the situation.

Barbara had been processing invoices for a long time, and she was pretty good at it. Over the last year, however, Barbara began having difficulty seeing the printing on the invoices. In fact, she was noticing that it was harder to see everything. It was difficult for her to admit, but she finally broke down and got some reading glasses. The new glasses helped some, but it still seemed to be taking twice the time to process each invoice. She was feeling bad about her performance and bad about getting older. To make things worse, the sales department had started using a new invoice that had even smaller writing than the previous invoices. Barbara found herself squinting to see the invoice, squinting to see her computer screen, and squinting to see who was calling her when she heard her name from across the room.

Barbara had to stay late almost every night to finish her work, and this was causing some scheduling strain at home. She was getting increasingly frustrated—even more so because nobody in leadership noticed that she was struggling. One evening when Barbara was working late, Tom had stopped by her desk. Tom said, "I've seen you working late quite a bit these days—thank you for your effort." Barbara forced a chuckle and said, "yes, I wish we had a better way to process these invoices." Tom replied, "well, we'll have to look into that. Good night— don't stay too late."

The next day, Barbara looked up several times and saw Tom peering over in her direction. She felt relieved that he would finally be focusing on making this invoicing process easier so she could be more efficient. Several weeks went by, however, and nothing seemed to be changing. Tom never said anything about it again. One evening, Barbara left several invoices unfinished on her desk. Still nothing from Tom. She couldn't believe it. She knew that Tom understood the problems she was facing. She had mentioned it to him, and she had complained to several of her co-workers. She was sure one of them would have advocated for her and mentioned it to Tom. She concluded that Tom didn't think that being able to do her job efficiently and comfortably was important. Barbara decided she would only process ten invoices each day. That should show Tom that something was broken.

A week later, she was sitting in Tom's office, and he was telling her that she was not meeting her quota. Barbara was furious. Tom knew what the problem was, but now she understood for sure that he was unwilling to do anything about it. When Tom finished speaking, Barbara said, "Okay," and walked out. She was more determined than ever to process no more than ten invoices each day. She knew how human resources policy worked. They would have to give her several written warnings before they could fire her. By that time, someone above Tom would notice his apathy toward his team members. They might even get rid of Tom and bring in a new manager who would care about the people in the department.

Well, as in the scenario from the previous section, I'm sure you can spot many places where this situation went off the rails and many ways the people involved might have avoided the misunderstandings. This is especially true because, as with Jim, Barbara's impression of the situation was not necessarily accurate. Tom had not noticed her vision problems. He was younger than her, and it just wasn't obvious to him that many people have problems with their close-up vision when they get a little older. And Barbara had never really sat down and explained it to him. Also, the night Tom spoke with Barbara, when she was working late, he had said he'd look into the invoice issue. But the truth is, it was the end of the day, and he was trying to get home to coach his son's soccer team. Though the conversation felt like a serious discussion to Barbara, it just felt like small talk to Tom. By the next day, he had forgotten it had taken place at all. Barbara, however, thought she had finally gotten up the nerve to tell Tom how she felt. Now the ball was in his court—she was waiting on him. When she thought that Tom was looking over at her thinking of ways to make her life better, it was just wishful thinking. Tom had just been looking around at the team every so often as he always did.

These misunderstandings seem almost ridiculous as we observe them. But I have seen things unfold in very similar ways. People misunderstand each other profoundly, and I assure you that this scenario is not at all farfetched. The point is that Barbara was frustrated by a problem she was encountering. Consequently, she complained to several co-workers about Tom and the company, convinced that they did not value equipping their employees to do their jobs well. Certainly, Tom might have done a better job cluing-in to Barbara's frustration, but he was a relatively inexperienced manager who hadn't gotten any leadership training when he was promoted.

In Chapters Eight, Nine, and Ten, we'll discuss some practical ways this might have been avoided. For now, let's just acknowledge that a major reason people complain is that they are frustrated by a problem they are encountering. To the extent that this problem is not quickly resolved, they will likely complain more.

# Being in Pain

A third reason people complain is that they are in pain.

When people are in pain, they respond to that pain in different ways—crying, yelling, silent stoicism, and so on. Complaining in some form is frequently part of this mix of responses.

I'm not at all being critical of those who complain because they are in pain. It is completely understandable. When people are suffering, they become disoriented, worn down, and hyper-focused on the thing that is causing them pain. That's true of most of us, so it's not fair to criticize. We should show compassion, patience, and understanding toward people who are suffering.

But again, we are trying to understand the reasons people complain *so that* we can do something constructive about the problem to which the complaining points. If a person is complaining because she is in some pain, addressing the source of that pain can be an important way of alleviating her suffering. And that is a compassionate thing to do.

With that in mind, let me provide some additional insights into this story of Jane, Jim's supervisor. Recall that Jim had sat in Jane's meeting scowling with his arms crossed. When Jane encouraged him to contribute, he said, "nope!" When she invited him to a private meeting afterward to try to understand why he wasn't contributing during the meeting, he coldly told her it was because he had nothing to say.

Jim's behavior in Jane's group meeting and the one-on-one she had with him afterward was rude and inappropriate—no doubt about that. I'm not excusing Jim's behavior, but recall that Jim was feeling helpless.

Nevertheless, Jim's behavior hurt Jane. Consequently, right after her one-on-one meeting with Jim, Jane walked straight into Sally's office and complained about Jim (Sally was the vice president of Jane's division). In this case, Jane was complaining because she was in pain. I'll explain.

Five years ago, Jane was hired into the organization by Phil. Phil had been mentoring Jane ever since she joined the organization. She felt a deep loyalty to him.

A couple of days before her painful meeting with Jim, Phil called Jane into his office and told her that Tony had left the organization unexpectedly. Phil asked Jane if she wanted to take Tony's place. Jane was thrilled. She had always wanted a shot at management. She too thought Tony was a tyrannical manager, and she was determined to be an inclusive leader that highly valued the input of her employees. In fact, that's why she had called the meeting where Jim sat scowling with his arms crossed.

As Jane was driving to work on the morning that was to be her first day leading the department, she got a phone call from Sally. Sally dropped a bomb on Jane. She explained that Phil had been suspected of embezzling money from the organization. Tony had also been involved, and that is why the organization had abruptly let him go. There was a criminal investigation underway. Since Jane had been close to Phil, she was under suspicion. Sally explained that the investigators wanted to question her that afternoon.

Jane was devastated. Her mentor Phil had been accused of doing something she never expected he could do. And now, she was under suspicion because of her close relationship to him. She knew she hadn't done anything illegal, but what if they produced some evidence that falsely accused her? She drove around aimlessly for two hours before coming into the office mid-morning.

When she arrived, she checked her messages. Sure enough, a detective from the local police had called to set up an interview with her later that day. As she was preparing herself emotionally to call him back, that's when Jim poked his head in her door. She felt so dead inside that she was barely able to say, "Can I help you?" When Jim asked to share his ideas with her, his request barely registered. All Jane knew was that she had no energy to engage with anyone about anything at that moment.

Jane took the next day off. She spent the morning crying on the couch in her pajamas. Around noon, something cleared for her. She decided that she was not going to let all of this derail her from leading the department well. The situation with Phil was a tragedy, but she would lick her wounds and move on. She wasn't guilty of anything criminal, so she had nothing to worry about. Her new team needed her, and she hadn't even met with them yet.

Jane washed her face and sat down to send an e-mail to her team, inviting them to a meeting the next day. She wanted to make it clear that she valued each of them and was determined to have a collaborative leadership approach.

At the meeting the next day, Jane felt good about the discussion. She couldn't tell anyone what was going on with the investigation, and Phil's departure had not yet been announced. But she did try to convey her excitement to be working with each of them. She couldn't understand why Jim seemed so cold and withdrawn. Wasn't he the one who poked his head in her door two days ago?

Jane was in pain when she went to Sally to complain about Jim. Her emotions had been on a roller coaster for the last several days. She was thrilled when Phil had promoted her to direct the business unit, but also nervous about whether her team would embrace her as a leader. Then she was crushed when Phil was accused of embezzling and terrified to learn that someone was investigating her. She was tormented by guilt for having ignored her new team while she grieved and got her head together. Did she blow her opportunity to win them over? Would they ever respect her? She had climbed out of the emotional hole and found the strength and courage she needed to lead. She finally convinced herself that she could start again with the team and be the leader they needed. With renewed optimism and vigor overpowering her doubts, she met with the team. Her fears of them rejecting her leadership were allayed when they responded well. But there was one member of the team who looked at her with folded arms and cynical eyes that said, "I see right through you; you'll never be a leader; you fall apart at the first sign of trouble; the only reason they gave you this position is that they were desperate!"

Frantically, Jane had called Jim into a private meeting. She had to know that she could win him over—only then would she be able to counter the doubts that haunted her. But Jim wasn't giving her a chance. Nothing she said seemed to win him over. She had heard how one team member could poison the others against a leader. She had just experienced the relief of feeling she had won over the team. Now Jim threatened that relief. She would endure the pain of rejection after all! All of this was causing Jane pain as she complained to Sally.

As observers, we know that most of this was not Jane's fault. Dealing with difficult team members on occasion is an unfortunate part of leadership. And, since we know what was really going on with Jim, we can surmise that Jane would likely have been able to win him over—and probably even endear herself to him as a boss—once she cleared up a few misunderstandings. Nevertheless, when we are in pain, we don't tend to think that straight. In Chapters Eleven and Twelve, we'll discuss some practical ways Jane might have processed this emotional messiness. For now, let's just observe that a major reason people complain is that they are experiencing pain.

## Having a Bad Attitude

Sometimes, it's not so much that people feel helpless, are frustrated by a problem, or are in pain. Sometimes, complaining has more to do with a person's character, habits, and outlook on life. This fourth reason people complain is that they have a bad attitude.

I have made this the last reason on purpose. It is tempting for us to treat complaining as simply the evidence of a bad attitude. When thinking about complaining in this way, our response is often just to tell people to adjust their attitude and stop complaining. If they don't respond positively, we can easily get into a contest of wills where we try to threaten them in some way with consequences if they do not change their attitude and stop complaining.

As we have seen from the other examples, however, there are a lot of other reasons that people complain. Threatening tends to either exacerbate the complaining or drive it underground. Neither option eliminates the complaining. So, we must consider other reasons for the complaining before we assume that the person has a bad attitude. We need to employ the right solutions, and this depends upon the reason for the complaining.

With those qualifications, however, it is important to acknowledge that sometimes the primary reason people complain *is* a bad attitude. After we have carefully considered other possible reasons for the complaining, we may have no other choice than to consider this possibility seriously.

There are several ways a bad attitude can show up. Sometimes, a bad attitude is due to a character flaw. We can want to get our way. We can be selfish, demanding that things revolve around us, as if we are the center of the universe. We can be overly ambitious. We can want to take things that are not ours—things like money, salary, glory, credit, attention, and on and on.

Sometimes a bad attitude is a sort of bad habit. Complaining can have a self-indulgent quality to it. In other words, it can feel good. Like anything that feels good, we can be tempted to indulge ourselves in it. Or, it can be just something we do automatically, like saying "um," playing with our hair, or doodling. Did you know that scowling can be a bad habit? So can negative thinking, the tendency to always believe we're right, or that we can do things better than others.

The point is that people can complain for reasons they cannot blame on helplessness, problems, or pain. Let's re-imagine the scenarios with Jim, Barbara, and Jane, where a bad attitude is the most significant reason for their behavior.

In the case of Jim, the problem might have been precisely what Jane feared—Jim simply didn't like her. He might have wanted her job. He might have had a problem working for a woman. He might be the kind of person that likes to talk behind the boss's back and tries to turn the others in the group against her. He might just be a jerk. People with this type of character flaw exist, unfortunately. Sometimes supervisors find them showing up in their working groups, sucking the life out of everybody.

What about Barbara? Perhaps Barbara's goal truly was to get away with as little work as she could and still get paid for it. When her supervisor Tom began to hold her accountable, she protested even more. When she complained to others on her team, her objective was to convince them to limit their production so that her laziness wasn't as obvious. Sadly, some people have no problem stealing from others, whether individuals or organizations. They find a way to justify their thievery and sometimes influence others to do the same.

And Jane? What if she really were a tyrant who truly did not value anyone else's input? Maybe she was quick to judge appearances and quickly decided that she didn't like Jim because he was an older worker. Or, perhaps she was so insecure as a leader that she discouraged input from others and took credit for their ideas when they came up with something good. Maybe she only wanted a team of sycophants and tried to get anyone removed who threatened her ego in any way. Maybe that was her goal when she complained to Sally about Jim. Tragically, these leaders exist, and they extend their misery-making to many who find themselves under their bailiwick.

Even if a person does have a bad attitude, however, threats alone are rarely effective. In Chapters Eleven and Twelve, we'll discuss some practical measures you can take when a bad attitude is the suspected root of the problem. For now, we'll just acknowledge that complaining can be the result of a bad attitude.

# Questions for Reflection and Discussion

In this chapter, we identified four general reasons people complain:

- They feel helpless
- They are frustrated by a problem
- They are in pain
- They have a bad attitude

1.  Can you think of examples from your own experience where you (or someone you know) complained for one of these reasons?

2.  Could you identify with any of the characters described in this chapter?

3.  Can you think of other reasons people complain that do not fall into one of these categories?

CHAPTER FOUR

# The Solution

Now that we've explored some of the main reasons people complain, the question shifts to what we can do about it. Remember, we're not just trying to stamp out complaining—we want to transform it. In fact, complaining can be a vital part of creating a 'no complaining' organizational culture. Yes, I am saying that complaining itself can be an important part of the solution. I'll describe how.

## A Practical Framework

My goal is always to be as practical as I can when trying to help individuals or organizations change. I find that you can teach someone how to do something (and that is an important part of the solution), but that's usually not enough. The problem is, in the heat of the moment, we tend to forget to implement the things that we've learned. Therefore, we need *signals* that remind us to act and *frameworks* to apply when we do.

I'll sum this up in a simple process that can transform complaining from something destructive into something constructive.

**The process to transform complaining is:**

ALERT → APPLY (filter) → ACT

The alert phase is where we notice that complaining is happening. That triggers the application of a filter through which we determine the reason for the complaining. Then, depending upon the reason for the complaining, we take the appropriate action(s) that will constructively address the issue(s) causing the complaining.

In this way, the act of complaining serves as an alert signal that initiates the process I will describe in the remainder of this book. You can refer to a diagram of this process in Appendix A.

# Alert

First, let's talk about the importance of a signal. If I were to ask you to tap your foot once every five minutes as you continue to read this book, I guarantee that you'd have a difficult time remembering to tap every five minutes. You might remember to do it the first couple of times, but soon enough, you'd begin focusing on the text (or daydreaming!), and you'd forget to tap your foot after one of the five-minute intervals.

Now, if I had a little red light that would flash in front of your eyes every five minutes, you could fully immerse yourself in the text (or in your daydream) because the red light would remind you to tap your foot every five minutes.

It's the same thing with creating a 'no complaining' culture. We could explore all sorts of ways to address the reasons behind the complaining (and we will). But they won't do any good if people don't implement them. And the reality is that when stuff is happening, emotions are churning, and habits are taking over, it's hard to remember to put what we've learned into practice. Therefore, we are going to use complaining as the signal that will ALERT us to move into action. This is a huge first step. Without it, the odds that we'll put the things we learn into practice get worse.

The way to use complaining as a signal to trigger a process is simple. Just *notice* and *acknowledge* that you or another person is complaining. That's it! Don't condemn yourself or anyone else. Condemning and being judgmental will not be helpful. In fact, it will be counterproductive because it will dissuade you and others from acknowledging that complaining is happening. So, when you *do* notice and acknowledge complaining, encourage yourself that you have taken an important (and often challenging) step forward.

It is important to note that this includes complaining that's happening in our minds. There are plenty of times we are complaining to ourselves, even though we never open our mouths. This kind of complaining is harder to notice, but you can get better at it as you become more self-aware.

Noticing that you are complaining can be an important first clue in tipping you off that something is wrong and needs to be addressed. This helps you begin to ask, "what's the problem? What am I concerned about? What do I need to do?" Now that we've noticed and acknowledged the complaining, we are ready to apply a filter to these questions.

# Apply (the Filter)

Now that you have been alerted to the complaining (i.e., you've noticed and acknowledged it), the next step is to APPLY a filter. The purpose of this step is to determine the most constructive action to take.

It is important not to skip this step. Again, I want this process to be very practical. Time, emotional energy, and other resources are limited. Therefore, when you act, you want to act in ways that are most likely to deliver constructive results. Applying a filter will help you select the best course of action.

**The filter consists of four questions:**

**QUESTION 1: "Why is this complaining happening?"**

This question will get you thinking in APPLY filter mode. You don't have to have an answer yet. Just begin to focus on the question.

**QUESTION 2: "Is the complaining happening because of one of these four reasons?"**

- I am feeling helpless
- I am frustrated by a problem
- I am in pain
- I have a bad attitude

If you find that the answer is yes to more than one of these questions, try to determine the relative significance of each. You might try putting a percentage by each question so that you have something like: "70% helpless; 20% problem; 5% pain; 5% attitude." In this case, your main focus should be the feeling of helplessness. When you address the feeling of helplessness, the other reasons may become insignificant. If not, you can then reapply the filter and act accordingly.

(Note that if someone else is the one complaining, you may be helping that person walk through the questions.)

**QUESTION 3: "What is the best solution?"**

Asking this question will start you moving from problem identification mode to problem-solving mode. The answer to this question will depend upon the reason for the complaining you identified in question 2. I'll explain each recommended solution in the ACT section below, but here is a quick reference summary:

- IF I am feeling helpless → THEN use Honoring Honesty to share my concerns with the appropriate people

- IF I am feeling frustrated by a problem → THEN employ the process of Problem Naming and Problem Solving

- IF I am in pain → THEN use Peer Support and Self-Awareness to pursue comfort, acceptance, and coping

- IF I have a bad attitude → THEN then use Peer Support and Self-Awareness to pursue growth and accountability

**QUESTION 4: "What are my next steps?"**

Within each of these general solutions are concrete next steps. The important thing here is that you identify the next step. Most people will not act if they don't have a very concrete action to take. So, speak it out, write it down, or whatever you need to do to identify the action that will begin the ACT phase of the process.

# Act

The final stage in the process is ACT. That sounds obvious, but it is the phase that takes the most courage, fortitude, and wisdom. It's where the process frequently ends for many people. Therefore, I can't emphasize enough that without action, little will change for the better. In one sense, it is much easier to destroy than to construct. But creating a 'no-complaining' organizational culture is a constructive process made possible only by action. So, the ACT phase is vital.

Which actions you take, however, will depend upon what you determine during the APPLY filter stage. There are three general solutions I will recommend for creating a 'no complaining' organizational culture. Each has subcomponents and details that I'll describe in subsequent chapters. For now, I'll only provide a summary of each, and the reason for complaining that each solution is designed to address.

## SOLUTION 1: A Culture of Honoring Honesty

The best way to address feelings of helplessness in organizations is to create a culture of Honoring Honesty. When people feel helpless, they often feel unheard and uninformed. Addressing those problems involves putting things in place so that people truly feel heard. That means teaching people to have productive interpersonal exchanges where everyone in the organization (leaders, followers, peers) can be honest with one another in ways that are respectful and civil. It also involves the creation, identification, and utilization of specific communications channels. Again, everyone (leaders, followers, peers) must take responsibility for making these channels work. Finally, this solution involves leaders learning to find their voice and followers learning to hear it. Most of the time, people feel helpless because they feel that someone else holds power. Therefore, leader-follower relations are subject to misunderstandings. Becoming familiar with these dynamics can help. We'll discuss this in more detail in Chapters Five, Six, and Seven.

## SOLUTION 2: A Culture of Problem Naming and Problem Solving

The best way to address problems that frustrate people in organizations is to create a culture of Problem Naming and Problem Solving. People need to have an opportunity to work the problem successfully. That may seem obvious, but the reality is that people rarely go into problem-solving mode when they encounter a problem. They more commonly take a sort of fatalistic approach, as if "this is just the way it is, so why bother to do anything about it?" That's why first naming a problem is so critical to being able to resolve it. Once the problem is named, people must know how to address it productively. Is it a small, medium, or large problem? What is the best plan of attack to resolve it? When can I realistically expect that it will be addressed? Who needs to be involved? Problems exist at all levels and in all corners of the organization. The creation of a Problem Naming and Problem Solving organizational culture requires everyone—not just leadership. We'll discuss this in more detail in Chapters Eight, Nine, and Ten.

## SOLUTION 3: A Culture of Self-Reflection and Support

The best way to address people experiencing pain and having a bad attitude is to create a culture of Self-Reflection and Support. When people are in pain, they must know how to comfort themselves and one another. Developing self-awareness through self-reflection will help because they will learn to identify the things that make them angry, anxious, discouraged, and so on. Likewise, a peer support network (whether formal or informal) can help them cope with the pain they are experiencing on the job. And, if people are struggling with a poor attitude, self-reflection can help them to be more honest about their attitude and gain insights into the reasons for it. Peer support, when done well, can also help people better understand themselves and provide some gracious accountability when another's attitude needs refinement. We'll discuss this in more detail in Chapters Eleven and Twelve.

# Questions for Reflection and Discussion

1. Do you think it's important to have a signal of some sort to help you remember to do something? How can complaining serve as an alert signal? Is it always easy to recognize complaining?

2. Take a look at the chart in Appendix A. Do you understand how to work through the ALERT → APPLY (filter) → ACT framework?

3. Think of some examples of complaining that you have observed. How would you apply the filter, and what solutions would you recommend for each example? (Feel free to use the examples from Chapter Three if you can't think of any others.)

# A CULTURE OF HONORING HONESTY

In Chapter Three, we identified *Feeling Helpless* as one of the reasons people complain.

**An important solution to people feeling helpless is to make sure they feel heard.** That does not mean paying lip service to some touchy-feely concept designed to disarm angry employees and make them walk away with a warm feeling in their hearts and a content smile on their faces. Rather, I am referring to the serious development of a system within which everyone in an organization has a sense that they can voice their concerns or ideas to the right people and that those concerns or ideas will be seriously engaged. This is made possible by developing a Culture of Honoring Honesty.

A Culture of Honoring Honesty is the opposite of a culture that tries to silence or ignore people. It is a culture that encourages healthy, productive communication where all parties—leaders, followers, peers—feel heard, not helpless. In her book, *The Fearless Organization*, Harvard Business School professor Amy Edmondson described the importance of creating an environment of psychological safety, where employees feel they can discuss whatever is on their minds. Kim Scott calls this idea "Radical Candor." Arianna Huffington labeled it "Compassionate Directness."

A Culture of Honoring Honesty is my version of this principle. In the next three chapters, I will describe what Honoring Honesty looks like and what I have found to be the most critical elements to practically implement it.

I have chosen the term "Culture of Honoring Honesty" deliberately. Each word has significance. "Culture" refers to something that is accepted and practiced naturally by all. That does not happen overnight, but it is the goal.

It's also important to acknowledge that a Culture includes a value system that not everyone everywhere shares. For example, some people admire those who use deceit to gain an advantage over another. Others would hold that employing deceit is morally wrong, even though it may be advantageous in some cases. It comes down to a difference in cultural value systems.

The point here is that a Culture of Honoring Honesty includes certain value judgments. We can't assume that everyone will agree with those value judgments. But if an organization is going to create this type of culture, it must unapologetically acknowledge a system of values that it considers to be right and expects its employees to practice.

The term "Honoring" modifies the term Honesty. It qualifies that honesty in interpersonal communications should always be for the benefit of others. It should never be an excuse to insult, wound, or manipulate. It implies that we must always acknowledge the dignity of others and treat them with respect.

Finally, the term "Honesty" refers to communications that are authentic and sincere, not duplicitous or manipulative. It's better to say "I don't know" or "I can't say" than to lie. We should, of course, exercise wisdom and sensitivity in our honesty. What we say should be appropriate for the circumstance in degree and form. Honesty that is untethered from Honor can quickly become destructive.

But this book is intended to be practical, so what does it actually look like to create a Culture of Honoring Honesty? In this section, over the next three chapters, we'll discuss three key components of such a culture:

- Productive interpersonal communications
- Vertical respect
- Designated communications channels

CHAPTER FIVE

# Learn Productive Interpersonal Communications

The first component of a Culture of Honoring Honest is for everyone in the organization to learn *how* to have productive interpersonal communication. In my experience, this is a seriously underdeveloped skill in most organizations. One reason for this is that interpersonal communication is a very soft skill. Therefore, most people don't know how to teach it, learn it, or assess how well it is practiced. Also, most people doing a job have some degree of expertise and competency in that job, and they generally measure their professionalism by their ability to do their specific job. But the consequence of not understanding the importance of interpersonal communications combined with a complacent sense of competence in their assigned task is that the serious development of interpersonal communication skills remains largely ignored.

What this means practically is that even though most organizations have an abundance of highly-skilled, educated, and competent people, these same people often have very poorly developed interpersonal communication skills. In many cases, these organizations have no idea about the degree to which these skills could be improved or how much more effective they could operate if these skills were better developed.

The interpersonal communication skills I will discuss in this chapter could apply to a group setting or between just two people. They apply at any level of the organization—to peer interactions and leader-follower interactions. Keep in mind that organizations tend to teach these skills to their executive teams but not to those further down the organizational hierarchy. Unfortunately, executives can sometimes see these skills as unimportant compared to their other responsibilities. The point is that organizations do better when everyone—from the executives to the line—commits to learning the same interpersonal skills.

Also, you don't have to use every one of these principles in every scenario. I'm not trying to create a rigid structure that feels forced and artificial. Practicing these principles may feel that way at first, but the goal is that they become habitual, natural, and practical over time. Nevertheless, the higher the stakes, the greater the potential for misunderstanding, the more sensitive the issue, or the worse the tension is, the more critical it will be that those involved employ these principles well. Remember, we're not talking about common, healthy, simple communications. We are addressing the things that cause complaining.

Before we move on, I'll say one last word about the advantage of having a commonly accepted and practiced structure and set of ground rules for interpersonal communication. A major reason that people tend to be afraid of confrontation is that they don't know how the other person will react. Consequently, when one person needs to confront another about something, he often goes to one of two extremes. He can either go into a defensive mode where he numbs himself to the other person. This generally means he will lack empathy and compassion for the other and is likely to hurt or wound. Or conversely, he will be so worried about the reaction the other will have that he will not be productively honest, or he will withdraw completely. Knowing that both people have bought into a set of ground rules and principles of productive interpersonal communications will take some of the fear out of confrontation—at least enough to get over the hump at times.

# Engage, Don't Run

Before describing some specific ground rules for interpersonal communications, it's important to draw attention to something I frequently observe in organizations. It is simply this. If people don't engage with each other, they will not have an opportunity to put these ground rules into practice, and they certainly won't resolve the things that need to be resolved. Therefore, the most basic principle of learning productive interpersonal communication skills is "Engage, Don't Run!"

This is simple but critical. I don't know how many people I've seen nod their head in agreement with this principle yet fail to put it into practice. I'm going to provide some tools that will help take away some of the fear of interpersonal communications and make them more productive. But for now, let me challenge you with something. Forgive me for being so direct, but here goes. If you run from a confrontation, then the fact that the issue remains unresolved is your fault—even if the other person(s) needs to be corrected for something. So, don't run, engage. You can do it!

One thing that will help defuse the tension when you are afraid of confrontation is to confess your fear to the other person. Say something like, "I know that we all agreed to address the issues that concern us rather than ignore them, so I am going to do that. But I want to admit that I am uncomfortable with confrontation."

If someone makes such a confession to you, it is important that you reassure that person. A confession is a moment of vulnerability. When a person allows herself to be vulnerable, she temporarily lets her defenses down. This is frightening. If it goes badly, she will be less likely to try it again. So, be sure to handle such honest confessions gently. You might say something like, "I really appreciate your honesty. I know it took courage to admit that and to even bring up this issue, so thank you. I will do everything I can to make our discussion respectful and productive."

# Use These Ground Rules

When entering a potentially uncomfortable conversation, it is reassuring to know that everyone in the organization has agreed to do their best to practice the same ground rules. This is helpful because there is always a giver and a receiver in any interpersonal communication. In practice, people take turns being the giver and the receiver as the discussion moves along. Therefore, when all involved parties are practicing the same ground rules, receivers will recognize what givers are employing and vice-versa. Thus, both parties will dance better together, so to speak. With that in mind, let's go over the ground rules I have found to be most helpful for productive interpersonal communications.

## *Develop Empathy*

Empathy is the ability to understand (at least to some degree) what another person is feeling, thinking, or how that person experiences the world. I could write an entire book on this subject alone, but I want to at least introduce some ideas here.

When you can empathize well, you will be better able to communicate with others, gain their trust, and show kindness to them. You will also find that the more you can empathize with others, the more you will be able to grant them grace and understanding, especially when they have offended you or let you down in some way.

It is important to clarify that empathizing does not necessarily mean agreeing or approving. But even if you don't agree or approve of something another person thinks, does, or says, you will at least have a better perspective and ability to disagree or correct the person graciously.

There are three techniques to practice when you are trying to empathize. I will summarize them as *Pause, Imagine,* and *Ask.* You might initiate these steps in the order I mention them. In practice, you will circle around and repeat the cycle over and over.

**The first step is *Pause.*** This is simply a reminder to take a moment to deliberately try to empathize. So often, we launch into our agenda or react unreflectively. Pause is a reminder to stop for a moment before proceeding.

**The next step is *Imagine.*** Here, you will try to identify as many significant factors as you can about how the other person is different from you. For example, is the person your leader, your subordinate? Different sex? Younger or older than you? Single, married? Does he or she have children? What are his or her political, religious, or philosophical leanings? What is he or she passionate about? What cultural background does the person have? What kind of personality does he or she have? What kind of job does he or she do? What is the person being held accountable for? Are you aware of any stressors in the person's life? These are just a few ideas. Some will be more relevant than others, depending upon the person. Now, as you consider the answers to these questions, try to imagine what is likely to cause the person anxiety, joy, sorrow, etc.

**The third step is *Ask* questions.** As you try to imagine how a person is feeling, thinking, or experiencing the world, you will inevitably realize that there are things about the person that you don't know or comprehend. That's understandable because you are not the person you're engaging. To better grasp these things, therefore, you must ask questions. The answers to these questions can help you empathize. When you ask questions, however, ask with respect and sensitivity. Acknowledge that you are not that person, so you know you'll never completely understand what it's like to be him or her. Emphasize that you want to respect the person's privacy, and you are not trying to be intrusive. But you care enough to want to understand the person better.

Developing empathy takes practice, work, risk, and experience. But it is a critical skill to develop when learning to have productive interpersonal communication.

## *Describe Your Thoughts and Feelings*

I just described the importance of empathy. When one person is trying to empathize with another, it is a much easier process when the person with whom you are trying to empathize is skilled at helping you understand his or her perspective. This is the other side of the empathy coin.

To do this effectively, a person needs to have some self-awareness. I'll talk more about self-awareness in Chapter Eleven. For now, I'll provide a couple of techniques that can help with interpersonal communications.

One of the most important things you can do to help another person empathize with you is to describe your feelings and perspective. Let's focus on describing feelings first.

I know that when it comes to talking about feelings, many people—especially in professional settings—cringe at the thought. Talking about feelings seems soft and weak or corny and touchy-feely. I want to argue that identifying and communicating your feelings is nothing of the sort. It is practical effectiveness. Here's why.

I promise you that whether you confess or otherwise show your true feelings about something, they are affecting you and the person with whom you're speaking. For example, if you're anxious about something, it will affect the questions you ask, the instructions you give, the things that are important to you, and so on—even if you do it with an unemotional poker-face. Therefore, if the person you're speaking with thinks that some of the things you are focusing on are ridiculous, your lack of explanation for your feelings is only going to exacerbate that person's confusion and frustration with you.

Now think about this. If you explain to the person *that* you are anxious about the situation and you explain *why* you are anxious, your behavior will make much more sense to the person. That means the persona will be less likely to be frustrated with you and more likely to try to address your anxiety in constructive and reassuring ways.

This principle applies in many situations. If a person hurt your feelings when she asked if you were certain that you'd meet a deadline, you would be more productive to explain that this question made you feel like she didn't trust you and that hurt your feelings. This is better than passive-aggressively saying something like, "Well, I *hope* I make the deadline." Conversely, the person asking you the question might explain that she was feeling anxiety because her boss was pressuring her about a project which would not be completed on time if you missed your deadline.

Do you see how this works? Explaining feelings is very practical for understanding our responses and helping others understand them also. It provides everyone with more information about the human beings (who all have feelings!) that are involved in the interaction. And that helps everyone empathize and respond productively.

This same principle applies when it comes to your thought processes. In other words, just as you can explain your emotional processing, you can also explain your rational processing. We don't all process things the same way, so we often must explain our thought processes to others. We might say, "the reason I did this or think this is because...." Or, we might say, "here is how that seems to me...."

The point is that the more you can help another person understand your thoughts and feelings, the more that person will be able to empathize with you, make more sense of your behavior, and engage with you productively.

## Don't Accuse, Ask

When we are upset or concerned about something, our first response is generally to charge in with guns blazing and begin firing off our assumptions. Resist that urge!

Going on the offensive is almost always counterproductive because it immediately sets off a cycle of attacking rather than understanding. When you attack another person, he instinctively goes into defense mode. Defense mode looks different for different people, but it's defense mode nonetheless.

For some, defense mode is a counterattack, where the person tries to bite back harder than you did when you voiced your initial assumptions. For others, defense mode looks like slippery maneuvering where the person tries to cover his tail with deception and misdirection. Still, for others, defense mode is essentially rolling over belly up and hoping the attack ends as quickly as it began.

What is important to note about any of these defense modes is that they are counterproductive. A counterattack almost certainly ensures that neither party will have problem-solving dialog because each is too busy trying to dominate the other. Deception is counterproductive because it invariably skirts around the real issue that the parties should address. And cow-towing surrender most likely fails to offer helpful counter-perspectives.

The better approach is, "Don't Accuse, Ask." Get your temper and anxiety under control and consider how you are going to approach the conversation. Think carefully about whether you have made any assumptions. If so, turn those assumptions into questions. Note—this takes a lot of discipline and self-control! But fostering an environment for productive dialog is worth it.

To put this principle of "Don't Accuse, Ask" into practice, here are some phrases you can use that can be helpful:

"Can you please help me understand … what you're thinking? Why you did that? Why you think this is important?"

"This is what it looks like to me … were you aware of that?"

"This is how I'm feeling …were you aware of that?"

"This is what I was thinking … were you aware of that?"

Try using some version of these phrases when you have a concern about another person. None of them are accusatory, and none assume anything. Rather, they seek clarity and understanding. They allow the other person to respond to you productively.

## Be Productively Honest

Remember that we're talking about creating a culture of Honoring Honesty. The honesty part of that means—well, that we need to be honest. In other words, it's important to take responsibility for identifying the issues that need to be addressed.

Did the person offend you? Is the person letting you down in some way? Are you upset or concerned about something? Is there something that you want?

Whatever the issue, it's important to be productively honest:

**You are productively honest when you provide as much information as is necessary to give the other person a fair opportunity to respond to your issue.**

For example, let's say a colleague is constantly interrupting you when you talk. You ask him to meet with you. So far, so good. In the meeting, you say that you'd like it if the two of you could try to make your conversations more productive. He says, "Sure, what do you think we need to do?" You respond, "I think we should try to listen to each other better." He says, "I agree, let's do that." But the next time you talk, he continues to interrupt you.

In this case, you weren't productively honest. In other words, you didn't give him enough information so that he could really correct the problem. It's important to own the fact that if you don't say something clearly, it's your fault—not the other person's. (Hopefully, I'm being productively honest here!)

Rather, a more productively honest statement might have been to add something like, "When we're talking, it would be really helpful to me if you would allow me to finish making my point without interrupting me." Now, he has specific information that he can engage.

There is such a thing as being too honest. For example, you don't need to add, "It seems to me like you just like to hear yourself talk." You may think that (and you may even be right), but in a business setting, it's probably not a helpful addition to the exchange.

In my view, the best way to be productively honest is to be as winsome, sincere, and natural as you can be. If it's not that serious, then don't make it unnecessarily heavy. Keep it light if that's appropriate for the subject. It's helpful to remind yourself that you're not trying to be critical but helpful. You're not trying to condemn or judge. Rather, your goal is to be redemptive and gracious. You're not just "telling it like it is." You're trying to give the other person the respect of being honest with him or her. The more you do this, the more natural it will be for you.

Nevertheless, if you are especially uncomfortable bringing something up, you might start by asking for permission: "May I be honest?" That will at least give the other person a chance to grant you the right to say something uncomfortable.

By the way, if someone says "may I be honest" to you, don't get nervous (which is what a lot of us would do). Rather, get excited that someone is going to offer you something that you will have an opportunity to evaluate to see whether you think it applies to you. This response will reduce your anxiety and the anxiety of the person who asked you for permission to be honest.

## Show Respect

This principle should be obvious—but it's not. I see people overlook it all too often. I'm talking about using basic phrases like, "Please," "Thank you," "Excuse me," and "I'm sorry." Or, phrases like, "Would you mind...?" or "Would you be kind enough to...?" and so on. Simple, common conventions designed to demonstrate respect for another are frequently dispensed with as unnecessary or even counterproductive. This is unfortunate.

Thankfully, there are plenty of people that have a good command of these basic social practices, but enough do not that it's worth emphasizing again and again. Here is just one example. I was in a store recently purchasing some flooring. The salesman who was helping me was doing a great job. As I was leaving, I heard the sales manager bark, "Come here!" to the salesman. The salesman ran over to the manager, saying, "Yes, sir?" I felt offended by the lack of respect the manager had for the salesman. It would have been very simple to say, "Please come here" in a more civil tone. Yet, I observe this kind of lack of respect in the workplace all too often—irrespective of education or income.

The reasons people fail to show respect are varied. Some people think that showing respect is tantamount to showing weakness. Some enjoy feeling like they have power over others, and showing respect to another intrudes upon that feeling of power. Some people feel they are entitled to dispense with these niceties because of the position they hold. Some are cynical and consider these gestures to be insincere, saccharine, and sentimental. Some people are rude and thoughtless. And some are simply too lazy to put in the effort.

Whatever the reasons, however, failing to show respect creates resentment, suspicion, and distance between people. None of these things is conducive to productive interpersonal communication.

It's important to understand that using conventions of respect is more than just squishy sentiment. Gestures of respect, such as those I mentioned above, show others that they have value in our eyes. The master snaps her fingers at a servant because she thinks the servant is beneath her. The implication is that the servant has less value as a person than she does.

Many people throughout history (and still in some places in the world today) have thought this way. But this sort of thinking destroys rather than creates a culture of honoring honesty with productive interpersonal communications. The constructive approach is to make it clear to others that you think they have just as much value and dignity as you have, irrespective of whether the person is your subordinate, your superior, or your peer. These simple gestures of respect are an important part of conveying this message.

Let me clarify something before we leave this topic. I am not suggesting that you have to slip in a "please" every other word to the point that it cripples normal conversation. I hope it is obvious that in urgent situations, one needs to be able to give clear, simple, direct orders. In combat, for example, a sergeant yelling to a corporal, "Tell him to get down!" is not necessarily a sign of disrespect, but likely a lifesaving command. But most of the time, in a normal work environment, we can give orders and slip in a "please" or a "thank you" here and there—as in, "Jane, will you please give me the results of that study your team did?"

## Recognize and Acknowledge Conflict Styles

When people dialogue together, one thing that determines the productivity of their communication is their conflict style—specifically, the combination of their conflict styles. For this reason, it is essential that each person is able to recognize and acknowledge his or her conflict style.

Much has been written about conflict styles, but I will distill it down to the basics I think are most important. First, when I speak of conflict styles, I don't necessarily mean to say that these principles are only relevant to interactions where there is a lot of tension between people (e.g., strong disagreement about how to solve a problem). While conflict style certainly has relevance to those scenarios, it also impacts common interactions people have when working together (e.g., asking when a colleague will be done with the copy machine).

With that clarification, let me give two general conflict styles that I think are most relevant (there are several others, but I don't think they are critical for our purposes here).

**Two conflict styles:**

- **Avoidant**—this is the tendency to avoid conflict (or anything that may cause conflict) whenever possible

- **Aggressive**—this is a willingness (or even a preference) to charge into conflict

Which of these do you think most describes you? If you're having trouble choosing between these two, it's likely that the conflict style you adopt depends upon the conflict style of the person with whom you're interacting. If that person is very avoidant, you might seem more aggressive. If the person is very aggressive, you might seem more avoidant. The important thing is to *recognize* the conflict styles of each person involved in the exchange *relative* to one another.

The next step is to *acknowledge* each person's conflict style. This can be helpful because when you name something, you defuse tension and open up opportunities. I don't mean to say that you should walk around announcing to everyone you meet that you have an avoidant (or aggressive) conflict style. But when you work closely with people, there will be opportunities for you to acknowledge one another's conflict style and the likely dynamics those styles will engender between you.

The final thing to understand regarding conflict styles is the dynamics of various combinations and the potential opportunities and risks of each combination.

**Here is a summary of conflict style dynamics:**

- **Avoidant and avoidant**—when both parties are avoidant, there is a great risk that important and sensitive issues will not be addressed with productive honesty. There is a risk that transactions will be slow because both parties are reluctant to stress deadlines. There is a risk that the parties will become more avoidant or passive-aggressive as they develop resentment toward one another because they are not addressing the things that concern them. The way forward is to acknowledge these risks and regularly ask one another very specifically if any are occurring. Give each other permission to ask uncomfortable questions and bring up uncomfortable issues.

- **Avoidant and aggressive**—when one party is aggressive and the other is avoidant, there is risk that the aggressive party will think that everything is going smoothly (because the avoidant party is not pushing back much) while the avoidant party will develop increasing feelings of resentment (because the avoidant party does not feel the aggressive party is leaving any space for his or her input). Eventually, the avoidant party will become increasingly stressed and likely resort to passive-aggressive defense mechanisms, like doing minimal work, refusing to contribute input, isolating from others, cynical comments, etc. The way forward is to acknowledge these risks in order to defuse tension. The aggressive party will often have to take the lead in regularly stopping and asking the avoidant person what he or she *really* thinks. The aggressive party must be disciplined enough not to interrupt. To help, the aggressive party can invitingly ask, "is there anything else?" The aggressive party can even ask, "On a scale of 1-10, how comfortable are you feeling expressing what you really are thinking?" The avoidant party will have to accept responsibility for speaking with productive honesty when he or she has the opportunity. It is important to note that when one party is a superior and the other is a subordinate, there is a good chance that you'll have this dynamic with the superior being the aggressive party and the subordinate being the avoidant party. This is often true no matter what conflict style each person generally employs.

- **Aggressive and aggressive**—when both parties are aggressive, there is a good opportunity for a healthy exchange of ideas, even when there is disagreement. The challenge for this combination is each party slowing down enough to *really* hear and understand the other. The risk is that each will aggressively argue for their own perspective without really engaging with the other party's ideas. In other words, they will talk past each other without really connecting; there will be a lot of bluster and activity, but limited progress. The way forward is for each party to practice the discipline of allowing the other to finish speaking and then ask clarifying questions. Note that in a group, aggressive types will likely do most of the talking, and this will feel like there is a lot of productive activity happening. It is important, however, to be sure to repeatedly invite the avoidant types to contribute.

In summary, then, it will be helpful for each person involved in a conflict to recognize and acknowledge the other's conflict style, the dynamics of the combinations of those conflict styles, and the things each must do to ensure productive communication in light of those dynamics.

## *Listen Well*

Listening well to others is a difficult but effective skill that can be cultivated and developed.

The term "active listening" has almost become a joke in discussions of interpersonal communications. You might hear people making fun of the injunction to "repeat back what the other person just said," dramatizing their point with sickly-sweet head nods and affirmations. I get it.

But please consider something. I have spent countless hours helping couples and groups resolve serious conflict. If I had only two or three tools that I could use to help them make progress, active listening would be one of them. When done right, it is one of the most effective methods of resolving interpersonal conflict. What I have found, however, is that many people think they know what active listening is, but few are truly able to use it effectively.

I'll first tell you why active listening is important. Active listening is important because it is very human. People like to feel like another person has genuinely heard and understood them. There is a loneliness to being you (because you must be you all by yourself!). This loneliness can cause grief, sadness, and anxiety for many. When people feel understood, however, they feel a little less lonely. That ingratiates them to the one who listens.

Also, people like to feel that they matter and have significance to others. When a person feels that another has not heard him, he feels the other does not care. Conversely, when a person feels heard, he feels cared for, and his affection for the listener increases.

Finally, most people hate the feeling of being powerless. When a person does not feel heard, she feels powerless. That often results in an escalation of resentment and aggression toward the non-listener. But when a person feels heard, the feeling of powerlessness diminishes. Even when the listener disagrees, the person sharing likely feels better about the situation than before. At least the listener can engage the sharer's thoughts accurately. Generally, this leads to increased understanding and trust.

With that said, let me give you some simple techniques to help you be a better listener.

Being a good listener is more than just being quiet and allowing the other person to speak without interrupting—though it is at least that. So, you can start there by simply practicing the discipline of *not interrupting* the other person but waiting for that person to finish speaking.

Beyond not interrupting, though, listening well involves *interacting* with what is being said in a way that demonstrates that you understand what the person is saying. You can even ask periodically, "Have I understood you correctly?" You can usually work this naturally into most conversations, and the person with whom you are interacting will appreciate you as a good listener.

When stakes and sensitivities are very high, however, it can be helpful to follow a strict *framework*. This becomes especially important if someone has come to you with a sensitive concern, or if there is tension between the two of you.

The framework is simple. *Listen* to the other person speak. When the person finishes, do your best to *summarize* what you heard the person say: "What I heard you say is...." And then *ask*, "Did I get that right?" If the person corrects you in any way, *repeat* the cycle by summarizing again with the refined information and ask if you got it right. Do this as many times as is necessary until the person says, "Yes, you got it right."

Resist the urge to engage at this point with what the person said. It doesn't matter whether you agree or disagree. The objective of this stage is simply for the other person to feel heard. Once the person says you have heard him accurately, you can then respond to what he said. Of course, now the whole thing should be reversed so that the other person is listening and repeating back to you what he heard you say. When this process is not working well, you may need to get a third party to help mediate and walk you and the other person through the framework.

By the way, please note that I used the term "feels" to describe the person's experience. It's important to realize that what matters is whether the person *feels* heard—not whether he *actually* was listened to. Therefore, it is important to ask whether the person feels heard. If not, keep trying. It's no good to simply say, "I heard you, so can we move on." Do the work to make sure the person you're interacting with feels heard. You will both benefit tremendously.

## *Don't Be Defensive*

If we're trying to develop a culture of honoring honesty with productive interpersonal communication, there will be times when people say things that correct, critique, or even offend us in some way. Often, our first instinct is to become defensive when this happens. But if this is going to work, we can't be.

Being defensive tends to show up in several ways. Can you recognize which of these defense styles would be your tendency?

- You almost reflexively begin listing off all the reasons why the person raising the concern is wrong. This will be typical of people with more aggressive conflict styles.

- You slink away in silence, but your mind is constantly ruminating as you desperately seek to justify yourself. You may even seek out others who you think will tell you what you want to hear.

- You immediately go numb to the person speaking to you. At this point, you're not even listening anymore. You might say things to get the person to go away like, "Ok," "I'll work on that," "I'm sorry," etc. But these are just deflections. As soon as the person leaves, you have buried the issue so deeply that you hardly think about it anymore.

All these defense mechanisms undermine productive interpersonal communications. There are better ways to respond when something is said that challenges us.

**First, *remind yourself* that receiving criticism does not mean you are being condemned as a terrible person who has no value.** A little trick that helps with this is to tell yourself something like, "This is a great opportunity for me to evaluate a perspective that might help me grow in some way."

**Second, *watch carefully* to see if you seem to be oversensitive to criticism.** A helpful clue is to notice when you employ some defense mechanism. There may be particular things to which you strongly react. Make a note of these. They are likely the result of some wounds or sensitivities that need to be healed. We all have them. As you discover these wounds, seek appropriate help. Self-awareness training and peer support can be helpful. I discuss those more in Chapters Eleven and Twelve. For some wounds, you may need to seek a more experienced counselor of some sort.

**Third, *repeat the concern* back to the person**: "So what I'm hearing you say is...." That will slow you down and help you avoid any of the defense mechanisms I listed above. It will force you to engage the issue rather than avoid it by reflexively launching into an aggressive or passive response.

**Fourth, *own your mistakes.*** If you determine that you do indeed have something to correct or apologize for, embrace it unequivocally. Just own it, confess it, and correct it. You'll be amazed at how freeing this is! One thing that will help is to practice giving and receiving grace. These principles reinforce each other—the more grace you give others, the more grace you will be able to receive from them. In other words, the more you can be gracious with the shortcomings of others, the more you will believe them when they tell you that they intended their critique to build you up not tear you down.

**Fifth, *you don't have to accept everything* that another person says if you don't agree.** But when you're unsure whether you agree, ask the person to allow you some time to think about it seriously. And then do what you said you were going to do—think about it and get back to the person! But remember this, if someone raises a concern about you, then that person feels concerned. So even if you don't agree with every detail raised, you should still work hard to figure out what is disturbing the person.

**Sixth, you can *acknowledge when someone is being mean.*** Unfortunately, sometimes people do not express their concerns with tact and grace. Sometimes another person's pain is directed at you in cruel ways. It's okay to acknowledge that the person's behavior was hurtful and inappropriate. When you feel hurt, take steps to address your pain, like taking a walk, praying or meditating, talking to a good friend, or whatever you find helpful. Then, when you're feeling a little more robust, consider this. Often your critics are the ones who will tell you important truths you need to hear, even though what they say is often exaggerated and mean-spirited. But don't discard it immediately. Weigh it, evaluate it, and then respond appropriately. If you've listened, repeated, and understood—and expressed empathy and concern for the person—it will be much easier to refute the critique if it is unfair.

## *Don't Be Mean*

This brings us to the last ground rule—Don't Be Mean.

**There's a difference between getting angry and being mean.** This distinction matters, because it's easier to recover from getting angry but much harder to recover from being mean. Everyone gets angry, though people express it in various ways. Some raise their voice, some swear, some stew in silent resentment, and so on. I'm not excusing this behavior. I'm only saying that it is understandable. Virtually all of us get angry at times, so it is easier for us to forgive someone else for getting angry—we know we'll need the same forgiveness from time to time.

**But being mean *wounds* others.** It causes pain that is harder for most people to forgive. I'm not saying that people cannot be forgiven for cruelty. They can. But it is a much more difficult process. And sometimes permanent relational damage is done. Cruelty is always counterproductive (not to mention immoral).

For example, raising your voice during a disagreement or storming off in a huff is getting angry. It is not good. Try not to do it. But it's easier to apologize for this kind of behavior and keep moving. On the other hand, saying something like "now I know why your spouse left you," "you're just a crook," or "you're a lazy fool" is being mean. Such words accomplish nothing productive and are only intended to wound. It is much harder to recover when you are cruel. It's never worth it.

**So, why do we resort to cruelty?** Understanding our motivations better can help us avoid doing it. There are several common reasons:

- **Lack of self-control**—when we are hurt or afraid, that hurt or fear often turns to anger in an instant. Then, when we lose our temper, we often want to seek an outlet to let it out. That can result in a temptation to wound the person who caused us pain or made us afraid. When we lack self-control, we can give vent to this impulse.

- **Intent to intimidate**—sometimes people are cruel because it is a way of intimidating and controlling others. This can be a deliberate and premeditated methodology or more of an automatic and intuitive way of operating.

- **Desire to punish**—this is when we feel that a person has done something wrong, and this gives us the right to punish the person by being cruel.

- **Desperation**—sometimes, we feel that nothing we do will get the other person's attention or get the person to stop (or start) doing something that's important to us. Our sense of desperation leads us to resort to cruelty.

- **Enjoyment**—believe it or not, more people than you might think enjoy being cruel to others. This might take the form of making fun of people, being deliberately rude or disrespectful, or acts of more serious cruelty.

Note that some of these reasons are deliberate, and some may be the result of blind spots. Whatever the reason, cruelty is always wrong and always counterproductive. Cruelty does damage that is hard to repair. It is far better to figure out how to avoid being cruel and find ways of resolving conflict that do not involve cruelty.

To avoid being cruel, develop your self-awareness and self-control. Realize that when you're hurt, you'll often become angry. When you're desperate, you'll often do desperate things. This is especially important if you're in a position of power because you can get away with things that others can't easily defend against. But even if you're under authority, this is no excuse to be cruel to the authority. Those in authority have feelings as you do. So disagree, be honest, be clear, but don't be mean. It will create more complications than it solves (and it's just not nice).

# Some Final Encouragement

Before moving on from these ground rules for productive interpersonal communication, let me encourage you with something.

These ground rules are only good if you use them effectively. This means first and foremost that you must think about them, try them, practice them, assess how you did, and try them some more.

I'm realistic enough to know that some people cringe at the idea of something that seems like another artificial, feel-good, hokey system that everyone is just going to caricature and lampoon. You might be surprised to know that I share your concern. I don't like approaches that treat adults like children, having them pass around sticks that indicate who has the right to speak or engage in other such belittling activities.

It's much better to teach grown people how to better communicate as grown people. Putting these ground rules into practice might feel a little forced and awkward at first. But if done right, they should eventually begin to look and feel like natural, respectful, honest, productive, *adult* conversation. And that's the goal.

# Questions for Reflection and Discussion

1. Do you tend to run away from uncomfortable conversations? What do you think of this statement: "If you run from a confrontation, then the fact that the issue remains unresolved is your fault—even if the other person(s) needs to be corrected for something."

2. Work through this list of interpersonal communication ground rules. Which of them do you think you do well, and which need improvement?

   • Develop empathy
   • Describe your thoughts and feelings
   • Don't accuse, ask
   • Be productively honest
   • Show respect
   • Recognize and acknowledge conflict styles
   • Listen well
   • Don't be defensive
   • Don't be mean

3. Are you uncomfortable with these ground rules? Do they feel "touchy-feely" to you? Can you see how they can eventually begin to look and feel like natural, respectful, honest, productive, *adult* conversation?

# CHAPTER SIX

# Cultivate Vertical Respect

The principles I outlined in Chapter Five apply to everyone in an organization, from the top executives to the entry-level. That includes peer relationships and vertical relationships (i.e., those between leaders and followers). But there are a few communications principles unique to vertical relationships, so I will take a moment to explore some of them.

## Learn to Hear a Leader's Voice

Leaders are often the ones initiating communications, so there is a lot of weight to what leaders communicate. Whether it's in a casual or formal context, when a leader speaks or writes (or even conveys something with body language), that communication carries a significant amount of influence. Furthermore, research suggests that followers (especially in younger generations) want to feel connected to and cared about by their leaders. But for this to happen, followers must be able to really "hear" their leaders when they try to communicate information, concern, interest, or even affection.

That means *leaders must find their voice,* and *followers must learn to hear it.* To put this another way, leaders need to discover and develop their own communication style. It's no good trying to turn a leader into something he or she is not. Certainly, some change and skill development are possible. But generally, it's very difficult to radically alter someone's personality. That is why leaders need to discover and develop their communication style.

This is an important thing to understand because followers have their own ideas about the type of leaders they prefer. When a leader diverges from a follower's preferred leadership style, that follower can easily become disappointed, and misunderstandings happen more easily. That can frustrate both leaders and followers.

To help resolve this disconnect, it is helpful for leaders to recognize their leadership style and be able to describe it to followers. Likewise, followers should learn to identify the communication style that they would prefer from a leader. That will help followers understand how their preference differs from their leader's nature. When leaders can identify and describe their leadership style, and followers can recognize their leadership style preferences, *this creates an opportunity* for leaders and followers to develop ideas that will help them compromise and communicate.

When people have personality conflicts, it can be disarming when both parties can name the personality dynamics at play. Naming things defuses tension and anxiety because it takes something hidden and brings it out in the open. Hidden things tend to make people nervous. Once people feel free to talk about something awkward and uncomfortable, the thing becomes less uncomfortable because it is no longer the elephant in the room that everyone is afraid to acknowledge.

With this in mind, I will provide a list of some common leadership communication styles. This is by no means an exhaustive list, and it may well be that some people have a sort of combination of several of these styles. But as you read through this list, note which styles best describe *your* leadership communication style, and which communication styles *you prefer* from a leader. If you don't find your style or preference in this list, hopefully these ideas will help you to describe those that better pertain to you.

Note that each of these leadership communication styles has strengths, weaknesses, and growth paths. Also, be aware that these descriptions are not primarily focused on what is going on inside the leader, but rather how the leader's communication style *appears* to followers.

## The Encourager

- **Description**—communicates in a warm, enthusiastic way. Uses a lot of positive affirmations.
- **Strengths**—tends to focus on positive things. Many people prefer a leader that they feel builds them up.
- **Weaknesses**—can ignore difficult issues or at least fail to address them thoroughly and directly.
- **Growth path**—know that encouragement is a great gift to share with others, so keep leveraging that natural ability. At the same time, be sure that you speak frankly about things that need to be addressed. Watch yourself for a tendency to dance around hard truths.

## The Writer

- **Description**—prefers to communicate in written form (e.g. email, memos, web posts, etc.)
- **Strengths**—writing well can be a powerful way to reach a lot of people in a large organization.
- **Weaknesses**—can be uncomfortable in unrehearsed settings requiring personal interaction with others.
- **Growth path**—continue to write and ask some trusted colleagues how to get more people to read what you write. At the same time, be certain you are not hiding behind your writing. As a leader, people will want to see you and interact with you at times.

## The Hider

- **Description**—prefers to issue instructions through someone else, rather than directly. May do this to avoid confrontation or to keep some distance from followers in order to maintain a leadership mystique.

- **Strengths**—this type of leader is often good at delegating duties and coordinating his or her direct reports.
- **Weaknesses**—Followers can develop a sense that this leader is off limits and inaccessible. This can lead to suspicion or a sense that the leader does not care about them.
- **Growth path**—determine why you tend to hide from followers. If you avoid conflict, learn to approach it in healthy ways. If your purpose is to create a leadership mystique, understand that this can be counterproductive in today's organizational culture where employees tend to want to see the human side of their leaders. Find some ways to periodically show that human side to your followers.

## *The Shouter*

- **Description**—tends to speak in animated ways that convey intensity or anger. This animation may be because the leader has trouble controlling emotions, believes that force will result in action, or is simply unaware that he or she is speaking in this way.
- **Strengths**—can often move people into action quickly.
- **Weaknesses**—followers tend to become nervous and intimidated and are less likely to share ideas that might be productive, especially if those ideas seem to diverge from the leader's perspective. Some followers become emotionally or physically unhealthy around this type of leader.
- **Growth path**—watch your temper carefully. Recognize that your strong personality can intimidate people. Acknowledge this to followers and apologize where necessary. Make it clear that you welcome their input. When followers provide input, go overboard in thanking them and engaging thoughtfully with their ideas—even if you end up disagreeing with some of them.

## *The Swaggerer*

- **Description**—likes to show off and dominate the room with a John Wayne or Robert De Niro sort of swagger. The leader may do this with a smile or with intensity.
- **Strengths**—can convey a sense of self-confidence that some people find reassuring.
- **Weaknesses**—can be perceived as arrogant and egocentric.
- **Growth path**—work hard to determine whether this swagger comes from true self-confidence or from an attempt to cover up insecurity. Try to relax and tap into the virtues of humility. Admit when you're wrong or unsure. Give credit to others. Laugh at yourself. Make space for other personalities to shine also.

## *The Intimidator*

- **Description**—usually tries to keep the other person a little off-balance. This may be through more overt forms of bullying, but it often shows up in more plausibly polite subtleties, such as intimidating eye contact or tricky questions.
- **Strengths**—leaders who employ this method are often effective in negotiations and investigations.
- **Weaknesses**—methods of intimidation often create stress and anxiety among followers. Consequently, followers are less able to contribute productively to conversations and problem-solving processes.
- **Growth path**—if you have the ability to intimidate, be very careful that you are only using it when you truly believe it is for a greater good. In most interactions with the people you lead, intimidation is cruel and unproductive. Also, if intimidation is natural for you, be very aware that you will likely intimidate others even when you do not mean to. To overcome this, you'll have to grant permission for candor to a few people willing to give you honest feedback.

## *The Disarmer Charmer*

- **Description**—usually well-spoken, comfortable, enthusiastic. Tends to have a crafted and upbeat response to everything.
- **Strengths**—speaks very well in front of others. Easy to like. Can often motivate, reassure, and win-over followers.
- **Weaknesses**—some followers can feel that this leader's responses are salesy and contrived. A desire to be liked and well-received can dissuade the leader from being productively honest.
- **Growth path**—if this describes you, you are probably a very good communicator. Use that gift to motivate and equip your followers. But be careful that you are not more worried about impressing people than you are about communicating what is best and most appropriate. Sometimes this will involve addressing difficult issues and correcting people. Learn to do this with your natural charm, but discipline yourself against becoming disingenuous.

## *The Anxious Reactor*

- **Description**—tends to make comments, call meetings, or issue communications in response to a development that causes him or her concern. There is often a sense of nervous urgency to these communications. Even when the leader is trying to seem calm, others can usually tell that he or she is very anxious.
- **Strengths**—willing to quickly address issues that need to be addressed.
- **Weaknesses**—can overreact without thinking through the issue. This can cause followers to become anxious along with the leader. Followers often respond with chaotic activity, rather than purposeful actions.
- **Growth path**—work hard to determine what is making you so anxious. Are you worried about what someone else will think of you? About danger? About financial loss? As you understand this better, do the work to figure out why you are so anxious and how to reduce your anxiety. Recognize that when you as a leader are anxious, this anxiety will likely infect your followers and make them less productive and less directed. Unless something

truly requires an immediate response, take as much time as you can afford to think it through before responding.

## The Commander

- **Description**—has no problem giving orders. Usually gets to the point with little fanfare.
- **Strengths**—very comfortable issuing instructions to others. This can be helpful in high-stress, critical, and fast-paced operations. Some followers prefer this decisive, clear, and direct style.
- **Weaknesses**—often has trouble turning off this direct communication style at times when more diplomacy, sensitivity, and conversation would be appropriate. Can come across to some followers as mechanical and dictatorial.
- **Growth path**—learn to distinguish between the times that your commanding communication style is most helpful and times when it can be off-putting to others. You may need to solicit feedback from trusted colleagues to get a better sense of this. Learn to slow down at times in order to create space for two-way dialogue rather than one-way commands. It is less efficient, but it is accomplishing productive benefits among those you lead. You'll still be able to command when that skill is most appropriate.

## The Reserved Professional

- **Description**—tends to maintain a poker-face that doesn't betray much. Even a smile is measured and controlled.
- **Strengths**—can maintain a sense of quiet, calm, confidence that can be reassuring to followers.
- **Weaknesses**—can seem cold and almost machine-like. Followers can interpret this as being distant, unfeeling, and lacking compassion.
- **Growth path**—learn to be a little more expressive at times. Try to be more demonstrative, especially by laughing even just a little bit more. Share a few appropriate personal insights into your

personal history or your present emotional state. Even a little disclosure will humanize you in ways your followers will likely appreciate.

## *The Story-Teller*

- **Description**—enjoys telling stories and using illustrations to make a point.
- **Strengths**—well-crafted narrations can be entertaining and effective ways to communicate.
- **Weaknesses**—these leaders often tend to process their thoughts out loud. This can sometimes result in rambling, long-winded speech. Sometimes followers have trouble understanding what they were supposed to take away from the commentary or what concrete actions they should take.
- **Growth path**—augment your story-telling ability by including a bulleted list of specific points or actions. Limit your comments to a fixed amount of time before you begin speaking and then watch your time carefully.

Again, this is not an exhaustive list of leadership communication styles, and some people might be a hybrid of several. But the goal here is to help leaders communicate better to followers and to help followers hear leaders better.

**To most effectively use this list of leadership communication styles, here are some simple steps to follow:**

- **Step 1**—Leaders identify which communication styles they tend to employ.

- **Step 2**—Followers identify which leadership communication styles they prefer a leader to employ.

- **Step 3**—Leaders and followers use the ground rules of productive interpersonal communications to explore together the likely dynamics of the combination of their actual and preferred leadership communication styles.

# Deal Credibly with Sensitive Issues

Because this culture of honoring honesty is intended to help overcome feelings of helplessness among those who are complaining, it is important that leaders credibly address even the most sensitive issues. One thing that causes employees to feel frustrated, suspicious, and helpless is when they feel that leaders are concealing important information. In fairness to leaders, however, sometimes there are issues so sensitive that they don't know how their employees would react if they discussed the issues frankly. Or, leaders may be dealing with things they are not at liberty to make public knowledge.

Let me suggest a compromise between employees' desire for honest responses and leaders' concerns about providing those responses. Leaders deal openly and honestly, even with very sensitive issues. Because, even when the news is bad news or the truth is hard truth, people will almost always prefer an honest, accurate, sincere response to a phony, misleading story designed to placate them. Employees, in turn, must engage this candor fairly, demonstrating that they can handle it and respond productively.

To help facilitate this type of healthy exchange, here are a few scenarios I see frequently that lead to employee concerns. I've also offered some suggested ways leaders might respond.

## *What If Employees Complain about Work-life Balance?*

There are a variety of reasons organizations may have a poor work-life balance. Perhaps, the very nature of the work impedes upon work-life balance. This is common with some forms of shift work in factories, law enforcement, medical care, etc. In these cases, acknowledging the challenges to work-life balance is much more effective than trying to minimize them or imply that people are being soft if they express concern. A frank discussion about how the nature of the work necessitates the work demands is better.

Employees will also be appreciative of being included in attempts to come up with a healthy solution. Too often, leaders try to resolve these issues without getting input from employees. When employees are part of the process, they often gain a better understanding of the difficulties in achieving the organization's mission in ways that would completely remove the challenges to work-life balance.

In some organizations, the reason for poor work-life balance is that the organizational philosophy demands an inordinate workload—long hours, weekends, etc. When this is the case, it's best to be upfront about those expectations during the hiring process. This also means the organization must be honest with itself about its real expectations. If the organization says it values work-life balance, but there is an unspoken rule that would penalize people who do not make dire work-life sacrifices, employees are likely to feel misled about the organization's values regarding work-life balance. Organizations that demand this kind of work-life sacrifice should accurately represent their expectations. Otherwise, employees will feel helpless and complain about work-life balance.

## What If Employees Complain about Their Compensation?

Most people would like to make a little more money. Some people, however, are quite discontented with their compensation. This is a frequent source of employee complaining. There are several reasons employers offer the compensation they do. Perhaps the organization has a low-cost strategy, and its business is dependent upon lowering costs—even labor costs. Perhaps the organization has a philosophy of paying lower salaries in exchange for certain other benefits (e.g., a flexible schedule, education and training, a career launch, etc.). Or, perhaps the organization is encountering financial difficulties that make it impossible to provide the compensation it would prefer to provide if it could.

Whatever the case, it's important to be open and honest with employees about the reasons they are compensated as they are. In my experience, most people understand when there is a good reason given about why they are not making more money. If they want to earn more, they may look for a position that pays more. But they will generally be understanding and respectful of leadership. When I find that employees become angry about compensation is when they feel they are treated unfairly or when they believe that leadership greed is the reason they are not being paid what they feel they are worth. If the organization is pursuing a good faith, fair compensation policy and truly has nothing to hide, it is far better to be as transparent as possible with employees about this thorny issue.

## What If the Organization Assigns Mundane Work?

Almost everyone must do work that seems boring, repetitive, or insignificant from time to time. The mission of some organizations, however, involves at least some employees engaging in work they consider mundane much of the time. Further complicating things, it may be that there is no good career path to work one's way out of the entry-level, mundane work. That can lead to employees complaining about the nature of the work. When faced with this concern, I have frequently observed leaders try to spin their response in any way possible *except* acknowledging that indeed the work can be mundane with little room for growth and development. It is as if acknowledging this would be tantamount to telling every employee to quit. The problem with this is that employees know better. Leaders who try to put a colorful wrapper around this type of monochrome work appear condescending, insincere, and insulting.

It's better to acknowledge the nature of the work and be honest about it. Just because a certain job is mundane doesn't mean there is no merit to working for the organization. It may be that the market is demanding this product or service. The fact that this organization provides it is what creates a job that otherwise wouldn't be there. In discussing the work honestly, leaders and employees might discover ways to make the work more tolerable. Perhaps, the organization can adopt a strategy to rotate good people through who are starting their careers, knowing that they will move on with gratitude after a few years. Perhaps, those that decide to stay may do so because this mundane job allows them a work-life balance that they value.

The point is that there is an answer for each of these scenarios, but leaders need to be honest, creative, and try hard to figure out how to make the best of the challenge. Truthful answers that don't insult employees' intelligence are best. Of course, if the real reason for employee concerns is that leaders truly lack integrity, then employees will complain, and they will have a basis for their complaints. For example, if leaders are truly trying to get as much as they can out of employees for as little as they can pay them and without regard for employee well-being, then leaders really can't tell the truth. In these cases, there will be a perpetual clash between leaders and employees. The far better option is for leaders to lead with integrity and a clear conscience. Out of that mindset, they can be honest—even about very sensitive topics.

In a discussion like this, it's important to acknowledge that there are some things leaders sincerely feel are inappropriate to discuss. Examples might be employee salaries, a planned merger or sale, a planned firing or hiring, and so on. My recommendation in these situations is to give as much information as is possible, and then suggest that providing more information is inappropriate and give the reason why. This is better than being deceitful, and most employees will respect that approach more than one that insults their intelligence.

## Cultivate Vertical Understanding

Followers need to understand that leaders frequently keep things close to their chest because they do not think that followers can handle the information they have. If leaders are going to be honest with followers, followers must be able to handle that honesty. It is not fair to ask a leader to be candid and then make that leader suffer consequences for that candor.

For example, if a leader tells employees that the market is in a downturn so there may be some belt-tightening, it is unfair for employees to turn that around and blame the leader for circumstances she can't control. Followers must realize that if leaders share sensitive information, the followers need to process it responsibly and maturely. If followers overreact, leaders will go back into ivory tower mode where they wall themselves off and make decisions high in the castle.

This principle also holds on a more personal level where leaders try to be more transparent and inclusive with followers. Many people these days say they prefer leaders who are authentic and vulnerable. But followers should understand that this is uncomfortable for many leaders because they worry that followers will interpret vulnerability as weakness.

For example, if a leader says, "I don't know," he worries that followers will see him as incompetent. If a leader says, "I'm worried," she worries that followers will see her as weak. That may seem ridiculous, but it's not. When leaders show vulnerability, they take risk. Most of them know this. If you are a follower, it's important to handle this risk with sensitivity by showing appreciation and giving reassurance to the leader.

Furthermore, many followers these days chafe under a relationship with their leader that feels hierarchical. These followers want leaders to employ a more collegial leadership style where leaders empower followers and treat them as equals. A lot of leaders are open to this type of leader-follower relationship (some leaders prefer it). Nevertheless, most leaders worry that if they give away too much authority or if they are too familiar with their followers, those followers might take advantage of that collegiality and lose respect for the leader's authority. Then the leader will be in the awkward position of trying to pull rank when rank is no longer recognized.

The answer to all of these tensions is vertical understanding. Simply put, *leaders should treat followers with respect,* and *followers should treat leaders with respect.* But each must try hard to understand the unique concerns of the other. Leaders should recognize that followers desire to be heard and valued; that they want to feel like their leader cares about them; that they can sometimes feel powerless as people under the authority of another. Likewise, followers should recognize that when leaders show vulnerability or adopt a more collegial leadership style, they worry that it will erode their authority. Followers must reciprocate by reassuring leaders that they respect their authority and will be careful not to put them in awkward positions where they feel they must pull rank.

I'll close this chapter with an example of a common conflict between leaders and followers, and how they might resolve it using vertical respect (facilitated by the interpersonal communication ground rules). Followers sometimes feel micromanaged by leaders, and leaders sometimes feel that followers want to keep them at a distance. If both parties would practice vertical respect, they could try to understand the other's perspective.

The supervisor might be anxious about whether the work she is responsible for will get done properly and on time. If it doesn't, her supervisor might be unhappy with her. Or, perhaps she needs to know the status of a certain task the follower was working on because she has other people to coordinate who are depending upon that task being completed. The follower, on the other hand, feels that the supervisor's inquiries are an indication that she doesn't trust him or that she doubts his competence.

A way these two can overcome this tension is to stop labeling this as micromanaging, and rather see it as reasonable communication that will develop and get better over time. By honest conversation, each party can help the other understand its perspective, and each party can try to allay the other's anxiety. They can agree on a frequency for when the follower will provide task updates. This scheduled update will address the leader's anxiety. When the leader needs something outside of the agreement, she can give a quick explanation about *why* she needs the update (e.g. "my boss needs to know," "forgive me, I'm just feeling anxious today," "something new came up that could change things," etc.). This explanation will address the follower's anxiety. Neither party has to make it a big deal. Just practice vertical respect for one another.

# Questions for Reflection and Discussion

1.  Do you think there are any unique dynamics to relationships between leaders and followers that differ from peer to peer relationships? If so, what are some of these unique dynamics?

2.  List some of the things you think that *followers* want/need from leaders? What are some things *leaders* want/need from followers? What kinds of things cause anxiety/stress in leaders? What kinds of things cause anxiety/stress in followers? How can leaders and followers use this information to understand and respect one another better?

3.  What do you think of the statement: *"Leaders must find their voice* and *followers must learn to hear it"*? Do you agree/disagree?

4.  As a follower, which leadership communication style(s) discussed in this chapter do you prefer?

5.  As a leader, which leadership communication style(s) best describe you? (Keep in mind that most people find themselves in some type of leadership position from time to time—even if it is not an official leadership role.)

6.  Do you and your leader (or follower) have different preferred leadership communication styles? If so, how might you overcome these differences and better communicate?

7.  As a follower, how would you prefer that leaders deal with sensitive issues? What concerns do you think leaders have when they must discuss sensitive issues with followers?

CHAPTER SEVEN

# Agree to Use Designated Communications Channels

When people feel unheard or uninformed, they also tend to feel disenfranchised, unempowered, surprised—and helpless. But effective communication is difficult. There are at least two general components of effective communication: 1) the interpersonal dynamic; 2) the physical communication channel or medium. We spent most of this chapter discussing the interpersonal dynamic. Before moving on, it's important to mention physical communication channels.

Physical communications channels become especially important for mass communications. Mass communications are exchanges of information that take place between larger numbers of people. Communication between two people (or a very small group of people is challenging enough). But when you need to communicate a message to or get feedback from larger groups of people, things get even harder.

Conventional wisdom assumes that communication is entirely dependent upon the person originating the message. In other words, the assumption is that nobody will *actively receive* communication. Therefore, the communicator must create multiple and repeated communications channels. This tends to be true for markets where the receiver is passive (not active). In other words, the receiver is *not* deliberately looking for the message in a specific place at a specific time. Entire industries have developed to offer expertise on how to diversify communications channels in order to penetrate the noise and get the message to sink into the targeted receiver.

But this type of communication is expensive and inefficient, though necessary where the receiver is passive. That's why marketing is so expensive. Whether the communicator is trying to get a receiver's attention about a product, a service, an event, an idea, a candidate, or anything else, that communicator must send the message repeatedly over multiple channels, hoping the message will eventually reach the ears, mind, and heart of the receiver.

When mass communications *within* an organization are approached in this way, much effort and expense go into issuing multiple communications over multiple channels. Not only is this expensive and time consuming, but many of the employees who are passive receivers do not actually receive the information from *any* of the multiple channels anyhow! Therefore, the communications effort is largely wasted.

**The *solution* to this problem is to turn *everyone* in the organization into an *active receiver*. Active receivers know how to receive a message and make an effort to receive it.** While this is virtually impossible to accomplish in the chaotic marketplace, the opportunity is present within the more controlled boundaries of an organization. Realizing these benefits is a process that requires some effort, however. For this to work, several process phases must be implemented.

**I'll summarize those phases as: Identify, Agree, Utilize, and Refine.**

# Identify

The first phase is to identify the communication channels your organization will use. This seems obvious, but it's not. In my experience, most employees could not name all the available communications channels the organization uses. They do not know the *purpose* of the communications channels of which they are aware. And they do not actively *utilize* all of the communications channels they do know about. Therefore, the organization must clearly identify the communications channels it decides to use.

There are many different communications channels available—email, intranet, paper memos, texts, business instant messaging software, suggestion boxes, in-person meetings, phone calls, video messages, and so on. This will be different for each organization.

**When identifying which communications channels your organization will use, here are a few guidelines that can help:**

- *Name* the communications channel and identify it as a communication channel;

- Clearly state the *purpose* of each communications channel—this is especially important if there will be different communications through different channels;

- Provide clear *instructions* about how to access the communications channel—the easier, the better;

- Clarify *who* is expected to utilize each communication channel.

Keep in mind that the fewer designated communications channels there are, the more likely people will use them. As you focus on identifying the communications channels your organization will use, you'll likely find that there are many. Therefore, you might need to decommission some in order to simplify.

**Here are some steps to help you optimize the communications channels your organization uses:**

- **Step 1**—Make a list of the *types* of communications that need to take place (e.g., state of the organization messages, new policies, employee feedback, project updates, etc.). Remember that some communications might flow *out to* employees, and some might flow *in from* employees.

- **Step 2**—Make a list of the various communications channels *currently* available.

- **Step 3**—Determine which channels people currently *utilize* most.

- **Step 4**—Determine which channels are *best* for each type of communication that you identified.

- **Step 5**—Determine which channels are *redundant.*

- **Step 6**—Now, use these information points to *narrow down* the communications channels you will use and what types of communication you will convey via each channel.

**GOAL OF THIS PHASE**—every person in the company (from executive to the line) should be able to identify each communication channel he or she is expected to utilize and the purpose of each of those communication channels.

# Agree

Once you have identified the communication channels that you'll use and the purpose for each, you will need to get buy-in from everyone in the organization. That means getting everyone to acknowledge the communications channels that will be used and agree to use them.

There are a variety of ways to do this. You might have people give a verbal acknowledgment after a meeting, sign a memo, or take a brief web tutorial where they check a box acknowledging that they've completed the tutorial and agree. The point here is to do something concrete where everyone agrees together.

**When presenting the plan to people and soliciting their agreement, here are a few guidelines that can be helpful:**

- Help everyone understand *why* this will be advantageous to them and everyone else in the organization;

- Set a clear date stating *when* the new communications channels will be operational;

- Make it clear that communications channels not identified will no longer be used for *official* communications;

- *Explain* the Identify, Agree, Utilize, and Refine process (more about Utilize and Refine in a minute)

Remember, if people have been a part of this process from the beginning, they are much more likely to buy-in. Of course, the irony at this stage is that you don't yet have clearly identified and agreed upon communications channels, so you'll have to do some extra work to get everyone in the company to participate. But the work will be worth it when you reap the benefits of the improved communications channels.

**GOAL OF THIS PHASE**—This is an agreement, so what's important here is that everyone understands, agrees, and takes responsibility for how communications will be conveyed within the organization.

# Utilize

People who have agreed to utilize the designated communications must utilize them. This is another one of those things that sounds obvious but isn't always. People do nod their heads in agreement and then fail to keep the agreement they made. That's not necessarily because they are stubborn. More likely, it is because they get busy and distracted, fall back into old habits, or forget.

Therefore, everyone in the organization will have to encourage each other to utilize the designated communications channels. Remind one another that unless everyone does it, it will not be effective. Keep in mind that there will often be a period of testing during which people learn that ignoring the agreement they made has consequences. For example, if the company issues a directive through an agreed-upon channel and someone complains that he didn't know about it, he might have to face whatever consequences come from not keeping the agreement.

Everyone must take responsibility for being active communicators and active receivers. Note that leaders and followers can both be communicators and receivers at times. For example, when the CEO wants to inspire the organization for an end-of-quarter push, this is an obvious case of a leader who is the communicator, and the employees are the receivers. But, when followers want to provide feedback about their benefits package, followers are the communicators, and leaders are the receivers.

The important thing here is that everyone is an active communicator or an active receiver. Therefore, it's not fair that the CEO expects the employees to hear her if she issues her end-of-quarter exhortation over Twitter, and Twitter is not one of the agreed-upon communications channels. That doesn't mean the CEO shouldn't use Twitter. It just means that Twitter should not be used when there is an expectation that everyone in the organization will receive the communication. Thus, the CEO is being an active communicator when she utilizes the *designated* communications channel.

Likewise, the employees are active receivers when they actively engage with the designated communications channels. Let's assume that the agreed-upon channel for this type of CEO communication is a weekly e-mail that comes out every Monday morning. Employees actively receive by deliberately checking their e-mail on Monday morning and engaging carefully with the CEO's message.

**GOAL OF THIS PHASE**—everyone in the organization utilizes the agreed-upon communications channels (really!).

# Refine

It is almost certain that these new communications channels will have hiccups that will require refining. Therefore, everyone in the organization must take responsibility for highlighting problems and making improvements. In the spirit of the main theme of this book, a good way to identify a problem with the communication channels is when you notice yourself or others complaining about them.

In Chapters Eight, Nine, and Ten, we will discuss specific steps for problem-solving. For this section, I'll just make the point that part of creating this new system of communication channels is identifying the communication channels employees should use to identify problems and notify about improvements. Employees should be aware of these communications channels and offer their suggestions for refinements.

**GOAL OF THIS PHASE**—clearly identify the communication channels to be used to report concerns about or be notified of improvements to the communications system. When anyone in the organization sees something about the communications system that needs to be improved, that person takes the designated steps to improve it, and the system responds and refines.

# Questions for Reflection and Discussion

1. What are some of the challenges with mass communications (i.e., communicating with many people at a time)?

2. List as many forms of internal mass communications as you can think of that occur within your organization (remember, communications can flow from leaders to followers, followers to leaders, one group to another, etc.).

3. What opportunities do organizations have when it comes to *internal* mass communications?

4. What is an *active receiver*? (see page 93). Do you think you have a responsibility to be an active receiver? Why or why not?

5. Discuss each phase of the process described in this chapter: *Identify*, *Agree*, *Utilize*, and *Refine*. What is the goal of each phase? How can you help during each phase?

# Solution One Section Summary

This section was about creating a Culture of Honoring Honesty to help address the feelings of helplessness that often lead to complaining.

Here is a summary of points made in eight, nine, and ten:

- When people feel unheard, they tend to feel helpless. Therefore, it important to facilitate effective interpersonal communication;

- Likewise, when people feel uninformed, they also feel helpless. People feel uninformed when they are unable to hear the voice of their leaders or when they feel leaders are not completely honest with them. Therefore, we want to help leaders communicate better and help followers hear the voice of their leaders. We also want to encourage leaders to be more transparent and truthful and to teach followers how to handle that transparency responsibly.

- Mass communication is difficult, so we want to facilitate effective communications channels that everyone agrees to utilize.

Of course, this improved communication will have many other positive benefits, such as improved morale, teamwork, productivity, problem-solving, creativity, employee health, and so on.

It's good for everyone!

# A CULTURE OF PROBLEM NAMING AND PROBLEM SOLVING

**CHAPTER 8: RESOLVE 'SMALL PROBLEMS' AS THEY COME UP**

**CHAPTER 9: MAKE A PLAN TO RESOLVE MEDIUM PROBLEMS**

**CHAPTER 10: IDENTIFY AND ACKNOWLEDGE 'LARGE PROBLEMS'**

Another reason people in organizations complain is that they feel frustrated by a problem. This might be a relatively small problem (like a broken printer) or a very large one (like the impact a recession has on the organization). The solution to this frustration is to acknowledge the problem by *naming* it accurately and by giving employees an opportunity to *solve* it.

There are many different types of problems that appear in various corners of an organization every day. These problems occur at every level of the organization in every department. They might affect just one person or many people in the organization. Some of these problems can be resolved by the person (or people) directly affected. Other problems need the help of other departments or leaders higher up the organizational chart.

What this means is that there is no *single* way to solve every problem. For example, if employees always rely on managers to solve their problems, those managers will not be able to keep up with the demand. On the other hand, if employees feel abandoned by managers whose help they need, they will become more frustrated.

To help sort through this, I want to offer a practical paradigm that everyone in the organization can follow as they address the many different problems that emerge. The *first step* is to acknowledge the problem by labeling it small, medium, or large. The *second step* is to engage the problem appropriately, according to the following guidelines:

- Resolve 'small problems' as they come up
- Make a plan to resolve 'medium problems'
- Identify and acknowledge 'large problems'

Small, medium, and large problems must be approached in different ways. Therefore, the first step in problem-solving is to determine what kind of problem you're facing and categorize it appropriately—name it! In each section, therefore, I will define what a small, medium, or large problem looks like. Then I will offer what I believe are the most appropriate and practical ways to address each type of problem.

# CHAPTER EIGHT

# Resolve 'Small Problems' as They Come Up

Small problems are opportunities. Because they can be resolved relatively quickly and easily, they can make employees feel empowered and productive. When leaders solve small problems, they ingratiate themselves to their followers. Solving small problems first involves determining whether the problem is truly a small problem (as opposed to a medium or large problem). Then, when it is categorized properly as a small problem, it needs to be resolved promptly.

In this chapter, I'll present a simple process that can help people who either cut corners or become paralyzed when faced with a small problem. It may seem a little strange to spend any time prescribing a method to solve small problems. We are tempted to just say, "Hey, you get paid to solve problems all day—just do it!" That is not an unreasonable response. But I want to suggest that a small problem is generally something employees encounter that interrupts their normal workflow (i.e., the normal problem solving their job involves). The problem may not be that difficult to solve, but if they can't get past it, it becomes a hump that will impede their productivity and cause them frustration. Some people are better at getting over these humps than others. Therefore, spending a little time making sure that *everyone* knows how to get over a small problem hump is worth it.

# What is a Small Problem?

The first step in addressing a small problem is to determine whether you are indeed dealing with a small problem. Here are some qualities of a small problem. Considering them will help you categorize the problem appropriately.

## *A small problem will continue to be a problem if it is not resolved*

For our purposes, a small problem is a problem that will *not* resolve itself but will remain a problem if you don't do something to fix it.

If the problem you're facing will resolve itself in a reasonable time frame, then it's probably not worth worrying about. An example might be a power failure in your building. You could solve the problem by acquiring a generator. But if it is likely that the power company will restore power by the time you get the generator connected, it's probably not worth your time to get the generator. Solve the problem another way—perhaps by working from a nearby coffee shop for a few hours.

Another way you might encounter a temporary problem that's not worth addressing is if you must perform a one-time task that you are unequipped to perform efficiently. For example, say your organization never sends out a mailer, but for some reason, it must send one. Some people get together to do the mailing and realize that they are not very efficient because they don't have mailroom equipment. While it wouldn't be a deal to pick up some mailing equipment, it's probably not worth it if you are unlikely to do many mailers.

On the other hand, if the problem that you're facing will continue if it's not addressed, then it becomes a problem that needs to be resolved. If, for example, the circuit breaker in your building blows several times each week, it's a problem to be solved. If it turns out that your organization will have to do frequent mailings, then the lack of efficient equipment becomes a problem to be solved.

It's important to consider this question when it comes to resolving small problems because daily work life is full of small problems. Many of them are frustrating but not worth addressing. Complaining doesn't help. It is better to work through them because you're probably not going to encounter them again. But if you determine that solving the problem will address something that would otherwise continue to be a problem, then, by all means, solve it!

## *A small problem can reasonably be resolved by the person encountering the problem*

Another quality of a small problem is that it can most likely be resolved by the person who noticed it. The more people you must enlist to resolve a problem, the more complicated it will be to resolve. Therefore, when you can resolve it yourself, you have a great opportunity. With that said, however, problems can still be considered small even when others must be involved, but...

## *If others do need to be involved, the person encountering the problem is able to enlist their help*

When you do need others to help you, it must be fairly easy to involve them. The people you enlist may be your supervisor or peers. The important point here is that they will respond easily to you and engage the problem-solving process. So, if you have a lot of tension with your co-workers or if they are not willing to help even with small things, then this is a larger problem to resolve (not a small problem). If your supervisor is hard to reach or very passive, then he is not likely to engage quickly and effectively. In this case, also, you have a larger problem to resolve. Even if your supervisor is accessible and effective, if the nature of the problem is such that he is not able to resolve the problem quickly, it is probably a medium or large problem.

## *It should take less than a couple of hours to solve a small problem*

The final criterion for a small problem is that it can be resolved within a couple of hours or less. The longer a problem takes to resolve, the more disturbance it creates in the organization's workflow. Even though problem-solving usually pays dividends in the long run, work is generally interrupted to solve problems. The more work that must be interrupted, the more planning needs to take place. It is also likely that resource owners must approve the time and resources involved in solving the problem. If the problem takes more than a couple of hours to fix, therefore, it is probably a medium or large problem.

So, if you have determined that you are facing a small problem, here are some recommended ways to address it.

(Note: if your problem does not seem to fit the criteria for a small problem, you should consider whether it is more appropriately categorized as a medium or large problem.)

## Resolve Small Problems Quickly

The strategy with small problems is to resolve them *as they come up*. That means moving quickly into action. But moving quickly into action is easier for some people than for others.

In my experience, there are two general types of people: those that move quickly into action, and those that have trouble moving into action. That may seem obvious, but the reasons for these behaviors are what becomes more important and interesting.

For example, those that have trouble moving into action, have trouble for several reasons (do any of these apply to you?):

- Some people over analyze the problem and get paralyzed
- Some people are afraid of something

- Some people don't know how to begin or what to do
- Some people are simply lazy

On the other hand, those that move quickly into action can sometimes take shortcuts that come back to bite them. Does this better describe you?

# A Small Problem Resolution Framework

No matter which of these tendencies you have, I have found that using a simple framework can be helpful. Answering the following questions and then acting can help both types of people give the problem some thought and then move into action.

## *What do I have to do?*

Answer this question in your mind, or out loud, or write it down if it helps. But, think about it and answer it with *specifics*. If it remains an abstraction, you likely won't act—especially if you tend to have trouble moving into action. Remember that we are talking about a small problem here, so you should be able to identify just a few things needed to solve it. If it truly is deeply complex, then it's probably not a small problem.

## *Does anyone else need to be involved?*

If you can solve the small problem on your own, then great. Being able to solve a small problem without anyone's help makes the process much simpler. But I'm not trying to discourage you from asking for help. Teamwork is a critical part of productivity. If others do need to be involved, however, either identify them in your mind, speak their names out loud, or write them down.

## *When will I do it?*

Don't allow yourself to avoid this question. If you can act immediately, then say it. If you'll address it when you get back from lunch, then state that clearly. Put in on your calendar or task list if you use one. If you truly cannot act without another person who will be back in the office tomorrow, then put it on your schedule for tomorrow. The point is, if you don't make it very clear when you will address this problem, there is a high risk that you won't do it. The preferred time frame is immediately. If this is not possible, then be certain you specify *when* you will act. For a small problem, this should be no more than a day or two from the time you identify the problem.

### Now execute

As obvious as it seems, the next step, of course, is to move into action. Whatever the first step of your plan is, do it! If you will take that first step, you'll be surprised at what you can accomplish. And you will feel great when you have resolved a problem that was frustrating you.

# Determine Whether Your Resolution is Temporary or Permanent

Once you've resolved the problem, you'll want to answer one more question: "Is this resolution a temporary band-aid or a long-term solution?"

As I mentioned, some people move quickly into action, but their solutions are temporary band-aids, rather than long term fixes. That's okay, *as long as* they recognize what they are doing. Of course, some people spend so much time figuring out the perfect solution that they never act. The best answer is to be able to move between these extremes, depending upon what it best. This is an art and takes time to develop. But it helps if you can recognize your own tendencies.

Therefore, when you resolve the small problem that you worked on, ask this question. If your solution is long term, then congratulate yourself for contributing some creative benefit to the world (no matter how small it is, it all adds up). And, if the fix is a temporary band-aid,

then figure out what the long-term solution should be. Then make a plan
it a long-term solution or re-categorize it to a medium or large problem.

# A Note for Leaders

If you are a leader and one of your followers comes to you with a small
problem, be sure to recognize it as the great opportunity it is. What I
mean is that a small problem for you might be a much larger problem
for someone who works for you. As a leader, you have authority and
resources that your followers do not necessarily have. What might take
your follower ten units of effort might only take you one unit of effort.
For example, you might be able to make a 30-second phone call that
saves your follower an entire afternoon of banging his head against the
wall.

Therefore, when a follower brings a problem to you that you can
categorize as a small problem, your relatively small effort will have a big
payoff in terms of the overall efficiency and productivity of the
organization. Additionally, when you solve a problem that a follower
was not able to solve easily, you will build valuable confidence and
appreciation among your followers. The faster you can solve the
problem, the more productivity and appreciation you will generate. Let
me emphasize again: a follower's bigger problem that is just a small
problem for you is a valuable opportunity on which you will want to
capitalize.

I'll make one caveat about this. You don't want your followers to
dump their work on your desk. Therefore, you really want to be sure
that you're not doing the follower's job. Rather, your role should be to
use your authority to create an environment within which your follower
can do her job. Also, consider whether there is a way that you can solve
the problem by teaching or empowering your follower to overcome the
hurdle that brought her to you in the first place. That's always the best
option if it is possible. Don't get in the habit of making people
dependent upon you.

When you've solved the problem and gotten your follower unstuck, you should touch base with the follower at an appropriate time to see if the problem is still resolved. This is an easy way to demonstrate to your followers that their problems matter to you. Likewise, followers should also give a quick update to supervisors in order to fine-tune the solution or just to let the supervisor know things are going well and to say thanks. This will encourage supervisors to continue to be helpful.

# Questions for Reflection and Discussion

1. Why is it important to be able to label a problem as small, medium, or large?

2. Define a "small problem." Give a few examples of a small problem that you've faced.

3. Do you think it is important to resolve small problems quickly? Why or why not?

4. Do you tend to move into action quickly? Or do you tend to hesitate and put things off? If you tend to hesitate, why do you think that is?

5. What do you think of the "small problem framework" on page 107-108? Is this helpful to you?

6. Why is it important to determine whether your small problem resolution is temporary or permanent?

7. Why are small problems opportunities for leaders?

8. Name as many benefits as you can that result from people in the organization learning to resolve small problems.

# CHAPTER NINE

# Make a Plan to Resolve 'Medium Problems'

Medium problems are more complicated than small problems and, therefore, cannot usually be resolved promptly. A medium problem might be something like the need to hire another team member to help alleviate the workload that is killing everyone. Maybe it's implementing a software system that will help the team better handle increased customer demand. Maybe it's fixing a maddeningly inefficient production process.

Medium problems are essentially projects that someone must manage. They require planning and execution with clear ownership. Because medium problems take longer to resolve and usually involve several people, there are more opportunities for things to slip through the cracks. When things slip through the cracks, employees become discouraged. That is why it's critical that leaders properly define and categorize the problem as a medium problem. They must make a clear plan to address it and keep everyone informed who is affected by it.

# What Is a Medium Problem?

The first step in addressing a medium problem is to determine whether you are indeed dealing with a medium problem. Here are some qualities of a medium problem. Considering them will help you categorize the problem appropriately.

## *A medium problem is a problem that can be resolved, but...*

For a problem to be categorized as a medium problem, it must be resolvable within some reasonable period. That period can vary dramatically, depending upon the nature of the issue—perhaps days or months. The important point, however, is that the solution is fairly clear (though details might still need to be determined) and achievable. Nevertheless...

## *It will take more than a couple of hours to solve the problem*

A medium problem requires substantial time to resolve. This creates some disruption to the organization because those involved in the solution (including the one who encountered the problem) must spend significant time addressing it. Consequently, these people will be redirected from their primary responsibilities, or they will have to take on additional workload.

## *The person encountering the problem probably cannot enlist the help of others without the approval or command of other supervisors*

Medium problems often (though not always) require the involvement of others. However, the person encountering the problem cannot enlist the help of others without involving other supervisors. That's because there might be approval needed for resources essential to solving the problem. Or, others who need to be involved may need the approval or command of their supervisors. For these reasons, the problem is too complicated to be categorized as a small problem.

# Define and Categorize

Determining whether the problem is small, medium, or large is not an exercise in pedantry. There's a real purpose to it. Remember that we are trying to respond to complaining that stems from people who run into problems.

Therefore, the important point here is to deliberately categorize the issue as a medium problem if it meets the criteria for a medium problem. Too often, frustrated employees bring up a problem while the people around them respond in a non-committal, lukewarm way. Maybe their eyes glaze over as if they didn't hear the comment. Maybe they shrug and dismiss the issue. Sometimes they say they'll look into it but then forget to follow up. Any of these responses will leave the complainer understandably frustrated.

The better response is to acknowledge the issue by labeling it very specifically. Naming things helps defuse tension. Correctly labeling the problem can also help set expectations about how it is likely to be addressed. Medium issues take some planning to resolve, but they are resolvable. The resolution might include fixing broken processes, acquiring new resources, new hires, etc.

**The first thing you need to do, therefore, is to find the person who can correctly categorize the problem.** The goal here is to find the person who can at least take an educated guess at labeling it. It might be you if you think you can muster the resources to solve it and if you think you have the empowerment to do so. You may know that you'll need approvals and assistance of others, but you're pretty confident you can create and work a plan to resolve it.

If you do not think you have the empowerment to own the resolution of the problem, escalate the issue to your supervisor, who should then determine if she can correctly categorize the problem.

# Make a Plan

Solving a medium problem requires a plan. They are generally too complicated to resolve without one. Almost everyone in the organization will have to manage some type of project from time to time, so I've included some basic principles here. This is not a project management book, so people accustomed to planning and executing projects will see nothing new. Nevertheless, these basic steps should provide guidance to someone who finds himself the owner of a project to resolve a medium problem. And keep in mind, the experience of solving a medium problem can be a great opportunity for an employee who doesn't generally manage projects to begin to develop those skills.

## STEP 1—Assign the Project Owner

Before you can proceed, you will need to answer these questions: Who owns the problem? Is it you? Is it someone above you? Will someone above you assign you to own it? Will you have the resources needed to resolve it?

As you consider these questions, understand that if you are the owner, but you don't own all the resources required, you might have to enlist the help of other leaders. That's okay, but you will want to be certain that the person who assigned you ownership will also support you with his or her authority. Assuming you are the project owner, follow these additional steps to create the problem-solving project.

## STEP 2—Create Your Task List and Timeline

- Write down *all* of the *tasks* that need to be accomplished. You might brainstorm this list with others who are likely to be part of the project.

- Assign an *owner* for each task

- Assign *deadlines* for each task

- Identify *critical* tasks—these are tasks that will take the longest to complete or tasks that will prevent the project from proceeding until they are completed. Pay special attention to how and when these tasks will get done. These tasks should be a priority.

- *Check in* regularly with all involved with the project for progress reports and accountability.

## STEP 3—Identify Short-term Workarounds

The project may take a while to complete, so try to find ways people can deal with the problem in the meantime. The temporary solution may not be ideal, but it will be better than nothing. People will be more patient with the workaround if they know that the more ideal solution is coming. Once you have identified the workaround, be sure to inform everyone who would benefit.

## STEP 4—Periodically Update Everyone Affected

There are likely more people affected by your project than just the people on the problem-solving team. These people are probably frustrated by the problem also. So, as the project leader, you'll want to identify them and regularly keep them informed about the project's progress also.

# A Note for Leaders

If you are a leader and you have acknowledged and categorized a medium problem, be sure to *do what you say you'll do*—or at least give your followers an update if something changes.

This is incredibly important with medium problems because, generally, medium problems need the help of leaders. And, medium problems usually take some time to resolve. Therefore, there is plenty of risk that leaders will get distracted by their many other responsibilities and will forget to do what they told their followers they would do. That's is understandable and very common, but it really undermines follower trust and exacerbates follower frustration.

**So, do what you say you'll do.** Be honest with your followers, even if it turns out that you have to recategorize the medium problem as a large problem. For example, maybe it turns out that an employee will not get a resource he needed because the executive team froze the budget due to a downturn in the economy. Without the resource, he cannot solve the medium problem. This may mean that the problem now must be recategorized as a large problem since it is not resolvable in the foreseeable future (see Chapter Ten). Discuss this honestly and clearly with your team.

**Be sure to give your followers pro-active updates.** Don't make the mistake of failing to respond just because you have no new information. From the perspective of the person waiting for an update, this makes it feel like you've forgotten them. If you said you'd give an update by Monday, then give an update Monday—even if the update is, "I have no new information."

If you don't have time to even think about the issue, much less categorize it or form a plan, then ask your follower if you can revisit it with her at a reasonable future date. The trick here, however, is to be sure that you then dig it back up in that promised time frame.

Remember, if you don't do what you say you'll do, whether that's categorizing a problem, making a plan, or performing the next step, followers will not trust you when you say you'll help. Consequently, they will begin to feel helpless and hopeless and start complaining again.

# Questions for Reflection and Discussion

1. Why is it important to be able to label a problem as small, medium, or large?

2. Define a "medium problem." Give a few examples of a medium problem that you've faced.

3. Why is it important to find the person who can categorize the problem as a medium problem?

4. Why is it important to make a plan in order to solve a medium problem?

5. How comfortable are you with managing projects? Do you think you could be the project owner of a medium problem and follow the steps under "Make a Plan"? Which steps do you think you could do well, and which steps would concern you?

6. What are some mistakes leaders can make when it comes to resolving medium problems? Why is it important that leaders avoid these mistakes?

7. Name as many benefits as you can that come from people in the organizations learning to resolve medium problems.

# CHAPTER TEN

# Identify and Acknowledge 'Large Problems'

A large problem is a problem that is not easily resolvable and likely cannot be resolved over the short term—and maybe never. This is an important distinction because it changes the way you think about the problem. Your approach changes from fixing the problem (as with small or medium problems) to learning to accept and deal with it the best you can.

## Examples of a Large Problem

An example of a large problem might be a financial crisis or a contracting market that places financial stress on your organization. Consequently, there is no extra money to increase wages. Since the organization is not expanding, there may not be opportunities for promotions—there may even be layoffs. Hopefully, upper management is trying to figure out how to get the organization through this difficult time. Still, the resolution of this type of problem is likely to be far out of the hands of most people in the organization, and resolving it may involve major strategic shifts with uncertain time frames and outcomes.

Another type of large problem may be an organization that requires some employees to perform a lot of tasks that are tedious—something like data entry of medical records, for example. Here again, the way these tasks are performed may change over the long term, but for now, these tasks are essential to the mission; there's no getting around it. They are tedious, but that's what customers are paying for, and someone must do it.

Jobs that involve stressful or dangerous work or challenging schedules could be another type of large problem. Some obvious cases might include certain types of medical jobs, public safety or law enforcement, military, or factory shift work. While things can be done to reduce some of the strain, the very nature of these jobs requires tasks that involve stress, danger, and scheduling hardships. That is not going to change.

I'll mention one more form of large problem that I see frequently. Some people badly want to feel like they are part of an organization that has significance, meaning, and purpose. They want to work for a great cause. Yet, many studies show that the majority of people are doing a job they feel has no meaning or significance. This gets even more complicated, however. Even people who start off working for an organization they feel has a meaningful mission often end up disillusioned as they encounter the everyday realities of their job duties. Consider nursing, for example. I can think of few jobs of greater importance than caring for people when they are suffering and afraid. Yet, the nursing profession has its share of people who are frustrated and cynical about their jobs. Therefore, I would categorize the feeling that a job has no meaning as a large problem, because very few jobs have some sort of built-in meaning that never fades. Most jobs will feel meaningless and insignificant at times—maybe most of the time.

## Acknowledge the Large Problem

When complaining comes as a result of a large problem, the first step is to acknowledge it. That means describe it and categorize it as a large problem. Once again, naming the problem accurately can defuse tension. Honesty is more disarming than disingenuous deception. I mentioned this in Chapter Six in the section about "dealing honestly with sensitive issues."

There are a few things that can help make this categorizing stage effective. First, describe the problem with some degree of accuracy and detail. Acknowledge how this problem affects you and other people. If you are a leader, your followers will appreciate this understanding because they will at least feel that you can empathize with how the problem is affecting them.

Second, state clearly that this is a large problem and remind the people you're speaking with what a large problem is. Remember that we must deal with small, medium, and large problems differently. So, if one person thinks the problem is a medium problem and the other thinks it is a large problem, you will not be able to seek a solution in a unified way. Therefore, be certain that everyone agrees that this is a large problem. Keep in mind that the only people who can truly categorize a large problem are people near the top of the organization. They are usually best positioned to know whether the problem can be solved over a reasonable period or not.

Third, if you are a leader (at any level) speaking to followers, identify what is within your control and what is not. Ask the people you are speaking to if they agree with your assessment. If you say that something is out of your control, but others think it is within your control, they will think you are trying to mislead them or silence them. If you're a follower, try to be fair with your leaders. Don't insist that something is within their control if it is not. Leaders and followers should spend some time working through this.

## Identify the Best Ways to Accept and Thrive

A large problem is not likely to resolve quickly—if ever. Therefore, the next step after acknowledging a large problem is learning to accept and deal with it the best you can and still be relatively joyous about your work. Several things can help you do this.

## Include Others

A critical part of this phase is to include others in the process. Remember that you are trying to figure out ways to help people make the best of a challenging thing—the large problem. But it's very difficult to impose happiness on others. A friend of mine who works a shift schedule recently experienced an example of how this should *not* be done. When employees complained about the schedule, management decided to change the way they did shift work. My friend told me that leadership never consulted the employees, and most of them disliked the new system more than the original system. Whatever you do, don't do it in a vacuum. By the way, if you are a follower and your leader does try to engage you in this process, make sure that you participate actively and constructively.

## Identify the Good

Another thing that can help in this phase is to try to identify everything that is good. Optimism and gratitude for what is good make the bad parts more tolerable. So, get together with others and make a list—write it down. The goal is not to paper over the problem or pretend it doesn't exist. We've already acknowledged it in detail in the previous phase. What we're doing now is making it more tolerable. Believe me, listing out all of the good things about the job will make the bad things more tolerable. Gratitude creates joy. There's a lot of psychological research showing that.

## Find Practical Ways to Make Things More Tolerable

Next, you'll want to get very practical and try to identify things that can be done to make the large problem less painful. For example, if the organization is financially constrained and does not have any paths for promotions, you might offer some skills training or personal development to help people grow. Perhaps someone on the team has some type of skill to teach others and would feel good about helping in this way. It may be cross-training in job skills, like accounting or computer programming. But it also may be something unrelated to the job, like relaxation techniques, painting, or book discussions. This doesn't replace a promotion or a raise, but at least people can feel they are progressing and growing in some way.

When the work is tedious, you can find ways to make a game out of it. A friend of mine recently told me of a game he played with a co-worker to see who could make the most sales calls and set the most appointments each day. Whoever lost, bought lunch the next day. This same friend organizes a game of company Jeopardy once per month that asks questions about customers, products, industry news, and employees. Find the fun people in the group and have them get creative. But, make participation voluntary. Everyone is different, so not everyone will be motivated by this sort of thing, and that's okay.

If the work is stressful, dangerous, or requires a disruptive schedule, you'll want to do everything you can to work with the people affected to figure out how to minimize the strains on life, health, and family while still accomplishing the mission. Organizations facing these types of challenges often have a culture that tends to minimize or ignore them as "just part of the job." I want to encourage you not to ignore them, however, because these strains take their toll in employees and their families, no matter how stoic the culture. So, be part of discussions designed to make things a little less dangerous, a little less stressful, or a little less disruptive. This is the responsible thing to do for your teammates and your family.

When the large problem is a feeling of lack of meaning or purpose in the job, there are a couple of approaches that can help. People want to feel that they are useful to others. Therefore, gathering and sharing stories of customers who appreciated the product or service offered can help. Also, if everyone gets in the habit of thanking people for their help (even when the help was routine), it can make people feel that they are contributing in some way. "Thank you Bob—you always have those papers filed the same day, and that helps me get my work done..." and so on.

When it comes to larger existential questions of meaning, you just may not find it in your work—and that's okay. Many people have heard the story of the custodian who worked at the NASA Space Center. When President John F. Kennedy toured the facility, he asked the man what he did for a living. The custodian responded, "I'm helping put a man on the moon." He was absolutely right, and it's great that he felt connected to the lunar project. But not everybody feels that sort of higher purpose from their job. When this is the case, it can be helpful to encourage employees to engage in meaningful activities *outside* of the workplace. The organization might find ways to be supportive of those kinds of efforts, like granting employees an hour of paid volunteer work that they can offer to a non-profit. Also, the organization itself might decide to support some meaningful cause. So, poll people for ideas. The bottom line is that meaning doesn't have to come primarily from the actual tasks you do or even from the organization you work for.

Self-awareness and peer support (which we'll discuss in the next chapter) can help with all of this. Self-awareness assists people in understanding what truly gives them joy and a sense of purpose. Sometimes people who are not very self-aware chase one thing after another, only to be perpetually disappointed. And sometimes, large problems cause pain (keep in mind that frustration is a form of pain). Peer support can be helpful to get through the pain because sometimes all you can do is get through it.

## A Note for Leaders

If you are a leader addressing a large problem, remember that clarity and honesty is key when you are working through ways to help followers deal with large problems. Followers will consider any of the measures we just discussed to be insulting if you, as a leader, have not first acknowledged the problem, because those measures do not make the large problems go away. But when leaders acknowledge large problems and categorize them honestly as large problems that aren't disappearing anytime soon. And only then do those leaders state that they nevertheless want to find ways to make those large problems less painful and frustrating. *Then* people will have more respect and appreciation for the leader's efforts.

By the way, if you are a follower, you must take responsibility for your part. If a leader tries to put these ideas into practice, don't be cynical. Be part of a team solution.

# Questions for Reflection and Discussion

1. Why is it important to be able to label a problem as small, medium, or large?

2. Define a "large problem." Give a few examples of large problems that you've faced.

3. Why is it important to acknowledge and categorize a large problem as a large problem?

4. Why is it important to learn to accept a large problem?

5. What are some ways you can learn to live with a large problem?

6. How can leaders and followers work together to face a large problem?

# Solution Two Section Summary

As we conclude this section, remember that the objective of these three chapters is to address employee frustration caused by problems they encounter. To address this, we are trying to develop a culture of problem naming and problem solving. Therefore, we first categorize the problem accurately as either a small, medium, or large problem. Then we take the appropriate course of action, depending upon the type of problem it is.

Think about it. If everyone in the organization does this, problems will be resolved. This is good for employees because they will be less frustrated (and complain less). It's good for supervisors because workers will be more empowered to take initiative and address issues on their own. And it's good for the organization as a whole because workers will become better problem solvers. This means that problems that would otherwise slow them down are overcome, so everyone becomes more efficient and productive.

And here's a great side benefit of the whole thing. The practice employees get solving problems will help them when they have to solve customer problems, internal efficiency problems, or create and improve products and services.

It's good for everyone!

# A CULTURE OF SELF-REFLECTION AND SUPPORT

**Chapter 11: Develop Self-Awareness**

**Chapter 12: Establish Peer Support**

In Chapter Three, we discussed two other reasons people complain: when they are in pain, and when they have a bad attitude. The solution is to create an environment of self-reflection and support.

Most people do not enjoy being in pain, but everyone responds to pain in their own way. If you stub your toe, there's a good chance that an expression of pain will come out of your mouth—perhaps a grunt, a groan, a scream, or a few choices words I probably shouldn't repeat here. A verbal response to pain is natural. It's the same when we suffer emotional pain. Often, our response takes the form of complaining.

It is important to note that complaining in response to pain is not necessarily the same as a bad attitude. Yes, sometimes complaining is due to a bad attitude, so we need to consider that and address how to deal with it. But a bad attitude should never be our first suspicion when someone complains; we should consider a bad attitude as a possibility only when we've ruled out everything else. So, assuming you have determined that the cause of the complaining is not primarily feeling helpless or being frustrated by a problem, the next thing to consider is whether the cause of complaining is some kind of pain.

To be sure, a bad attitude can *accompany* pain. But in these cases, the process of addressing the pain will often resolve the bad attitude. At any rate, threats to simply "stop having a bad attitude" are rarely helpful, except as a last resort. That is why the first thing to consider is pain.

The good news is that the solution to pain and the solution to a bad attitude are the same—self-reflection and peer support. Self-reflection helps people learn to recognize pain and better understand their response to it. To the extent that they have a bad attitude that needs correcting, self-reflection will help them recognize that as well.

Peer support can help create an environment where people can find some relief from their pain. When done well, peer support can also help develop self-awareness (the goal of self-reflection) and hold people accountable for a bad attitude when that is significant. The safety that healthy peer support can provide is an excellent place for the honesty that is essential to real positive change. I should also mention here that self-reflection and peer support are crucial facilitators that sort of grease the gears for improved interpersonal communications and problem solving (Solutions 1 and 2).

Before we move on to the details of developing a culture of self-reflection and peer support, let me offer some reassurance if you are a little skeptical. The goal here is not to create a therapeutic culture that encourages people to indulge in self-pity and make everyone around them walk on eggshells because they are emotionally unstable. But please consider—that happens anyway when you don't have constructive outlets in place.

Self-reflection and peer support, however, meet people where they are and then help them move in a productive direction. This is not done by ignoring problems, telling people to "suck it up," or by gingerly dancing around the temperamental person. Rather, you accomplish this by helping the person heal and grow—and holding the person accountable. That's why it is critical to have self-reflection *and* peer support together. They balance and reinforce each other. Self-reflection helps people understand their behaviors and motivations. Peer support helps people heal and grow. Healthy employees are productive employees that are more likely to stick around.

# CHAPTER ELEVEN

# Develop Self-Awareness

A culture of self-reflection is one where people regularly ask themselves: What am I feeling? What am I thinking? What am I doing? Why am I feeling, thinking, or doing these things? And what should I do in response? The goal of self-reflection, however, is *not* to create a bunch of over-self-analyzing neurotics. Rather, the goal of self-reflection is self-awareness that fosters resilience, health, and satisfying relationships.

In this chapter, I'll define self-awareness, describe how to become more self-aware, offer some important self-awareness techniques, and provide some practical next steps.

## What is Self-Awareness and Why Is It Important?

In my experience, a surprising number of people dismiss self-awareness as unimportant. This seems to be due to one of several reasons:

- They do not understand what self-awareness really is

- They do not think self-awareness is important—therefore, not worth their time and effort

- They think they are already sufficiently self-aware and therefore do not have to do any more work

- They are afraid of the process

Do any of these seem to apply to you?

I should mention here that I also know people who over-indulge in the self-awareness process, almost to the point of obsession where they can do little else. Neither extreme is healthy.

Whatever best describes you, please approach this section with an open mind. I will try to make the case that growing in this area can be beneficial to you, and I'll provide some practical techniques you can use to engage the process in healthy and productive ways. First, let's discuss what self-awareness is and why it matters.

## The Outside Person and the Inside Person

There is a difference between what I'll call the outside person and the inside person. It's the distinction between *behavior* (i.e., what's happening on the outside of us) and *inner experience* (i.e., what's happening on the inside of us). For example, we might smile and congratulate a colleague for recently receiving a promotion when on the inside we're boiling over thinking, "I deserved that promotion so much more than you did!"

Both the inside person and the outside person are important to consider. Sometimes we are quite aware that what is happening on the outside is very different than what is happening on the inside. Other times we assume that what we're experiencing on the inside exactly reflects what is showing up on the outside. That's fine if what is happening on the inside and outside are truly the same. The problem is that sometimes we don't understand how others perceive us (i.e., how we appear on the outside).

For example, a person might genuinely feel warm and embracing toward others, but those same people might think she is cold and disinterested. In this case, she is not aware that her inside person and outside person are different—she thinks they are the same. Therefore, her first step is to understand that there is a difference between inside and outside. And then she must learn how to convey that genuine warmth and openness to others through her body language, facial expressions, and tone of voice.

Another problem is that sometimes people don't understand how they are feeling on the inside. For example, a person may be quite anxious about a meeting, but he is not aware that he is feeling this anxiety. When a co-worker asks to borrow a stapler, he rolls his eyes, holds out the stapler and says, "Here," without even looking up. He blames his office mate for his rudeness, thinking to himself, "People are so aggravating!" He doesn't realize the problem is actually his anxiety about what others will think of his presentation.

## *Difference Between Self-Awareness and Self-Knowledge*

The terms self-knowledge and self-awareness are often used interchangeably. Both involve external behavior and internal experience. But there is an important distinction between them:

- **Self-knowledge** is understanding what we are like *in theory*;

- **Self-awareness** is being able to recognize these things about ourselves *in real-time*—that is, while they are happening!

We usually begin with self-knowledge but work toward self-awareness. That is why we can admit to someone that we have a temper and then actually lose our temper before the conversation is over. In this case, we have come to realize that we have a temper (i.e., self-knowledge), but we lack the self-awareness to notice it beginning to boil during the conversation, much less do anything about it.

It's important to recognize that self-awareness is the goal, but self-knowledge is the starting place. Understanding this helps us to be gracious with ourselves as we grow (and mess up!) and develop self-awareness. Yet at the same time, we don't become complacent. Rather, we actively continue learning to recognize and manage our feelings and behaviors, *as we are* experiencing them.

## Why is Self-Awareness Important?

Most of us don't do things unless we really think they're important, so let's address this question: Why is self-awareness important?

People do all sorts of things for reasons they don't understand—chasing success to win the approval of a parent, insulting others to cover their shame, intimating others because they are afraid, and so on.

What's important to recognize is that most of us operate on a sort of autopilot, instinctively responding to things we believe are making us feel bad and pursuing things we think will make us feel good. There is often not a lot of thought going into our actions, and this can create a serious concern for us. When we diagnose the wrong problem, we often chase the wrong solution, overreact to a circumstance, or make unwise choices.

Here is an example. A person may feel unhappy (a problem) and think he'll be happy if he gets a promotion (the solution). Consequently, he may sacrifice his own family to long hours at the office in pursuit of a promotion. But what if the real reason for his unhappiness is the need to impress his parents who burdened him since childhood with unattainably high standards? Notice that even if he gets the promotion (i.e., his solution), the real problem (i.e., his parents' approval) is still not resolved. Therefore, it is likely that he'll continue the same pattern of sacrificing his own family.

Notice this also—if he does *not* get the promotion, his world collapses in despair because his desire for the promotion was not simply a healthy inclination to work hard and advance in his career. It was to gain something far more vital to his existence—his parents' love.

Consequently, rather than working through the understandable disappointment of not getting the promotion, the intensity of his despair sends him into a severe depression that affects his family and his employees. He begins drinking heavily and alienating everyone around him. His wife eventually takes the kids and moves in with her parents, and three of his employees quit because they say working for him is insufferable.

I wish I were exaggerating with this example—or providing a rare, extreme case—but I'm not. I have seen this scenario play out again and again in a thousand different ways. The good news is that the more people gain self-awareness, the more they begin to understand what they do and why they do it; what they are feeling and why they feel that way. When this happens, relationships improve, judgment improves, choices improve, and happiness improves.

## How to Become Self-Aware

Before we discuss some specific self-awareness techniques, let me say a few general things about the process of developing self-awareness. The first thing to understand is that developing self-awareness is a lifelong process. Therefore, you must be gracious and patient with yourself and with others. I wish this were a quick fix, but it's not. Nevertheless, great progress can be made, and you and those around you will notice and benefit.

There are numerous ways to develop self-knowledge. One way is to participate in a personality assessment process. Some commonly found in the workplace are the Myers–Briggs Type Indicator (MBTI), DiSC personality test, CliftonStrengths assessment (or it's cousin Core Clarity), and Enneagram. Each of these has its strengths and weaknesses. I won't get into a detailed evaluation of each here, but you can certainly ask your human resources representative if the organization ever offers these evaluations. If you have an opportunity to try one of these, I recommend that you do.

Other paths to help develop self-knowledge and move toward self-awareness can include faith traditions. Many faith groups have their own ways of studying universal ideas about life, people, work, charity, and other big subjects. Literature is another source. One of the marks of great writing is a profound understanding of human nature. So, that book discussion group you belong to can be a great place to learn about yourself. Support groups such as 12-step programs and others are also great places to grow. These groups often have a structured system that takes people through a process of transformation with others who are on the same journey. Finally, if you do no other form of self-awareness development, the principles in this chapter can be a great start (especially if they are accompanied by good peer support).

No matter what forms of self-awareness development you pursue, here are some key things you'll need to practice for the self-knowledge you learn to become true self-awareness.

**In other words, if you want to experience real transformation, you *must* do the following:**

- **Learn to pause and observe yourself *in the moment*—**what is happening on the outside *and* on the inside? Note that this requires both remembering to do it and exercising at least a little self-control and discipline to be able to do it *as* it is happening.

- **Self-reflection—**ask yourself appropriate questions, such as: How am I actually behaving right now? What am I feeling right now? What do I really want? (As you learn the self-awareness techniques below, you will get better at asking yourself appropriate questions).

- **Get feedback from a trusted observer—**it is very difficult to notice our blind spots, but we all have them. So, we need feedback from others. This may come from a formal feedback program like a 360-review or an executive coach. Or, it may be informal feedback from a friend, spouse, peer support, etc.

# Self-Awareness Techniques

Now that we've discussed self-awareness in general, I want to provide some specific techniques you can use to help yourself and others grow. This is not a comprehensive list. Many full books are written about any one of these techniques. But I want to offer a starting place, so I have assembled a list of some things I see most often. I should point out that I am primarily focusing on self-awareness issues common to the workplace, not necessarily things like how to be a better friend, spouse, parent, etc. Nevertheless, all these techniques will have relevance to those areas of life as well.

## *Assess Your Level of Self-Control*

I'll start with this because it is the most urgent. People do things they regret when they lack self-control. Therefore, developing self-control is a critical first step to avoid making mistakes that are hard to undo.

But before you can address a lack of self-control, you need to become aware of your lack of self-control. Many people have no idea that they lack self-control, so they are already at a disadvantage.

So, ask yourself the following questions:

- Do you fly off the handle and overreact in ways over which you do not feel you have complete control?

- Do you hurt others, make things more complicated with your responses, or say things you regret later?

- Are you absolutely certain about how you affect others?

Keep in mind that this lack of self-control might involve obvious behaviors like yelling, sending angry e-mails, or making inappropriate social media posts. But it also may involve passive-aggressive behavior like subtle insults or jabs. The key here is to notice whether you have a pattern of doing things that you regret, especially if you felt like you did not have complete control over your actions. By the way, if you do think you have good self-control, but you choose to act in these unhealthy ways anyhow, I want to refer you back to Chapter Five and the ground rules for productive interpersonal communication.

Also, beware that some people might mistake silence for self-control. It's not necessarily self-control, however, if a person goes numb, turns inward, and shuts down. This is effectively another form of a *lack* of self-control because the person is unable to control her internal response. She may now be unable to do her job because she has reacted so strongly on the inside.

**So, if you determine that you lack self-control, what should you do?**

**First, understand and acknowledge that your lack of self-control clouds your judgment, hurts others, and causes damage that is not easily undone.** Take a moment to reflect on each of those for a moment. Do you want clouded judgment? Do you want to hurt others? Do you want to cause damage that seriously complicates your life in ways that might not be fixable? I have found that unless people have a very clear understanding of the consequences of their lack of self-control, they really won't do the work to address it. So, spend some time honestly answering these questions.

**Next, walk away if you need to.** Walk away if you think you are at risk of responding without self-control. That is better than saying or doing something you'll regret. Just be sure you come back and apologize when you've cooled down (walking away is better than saying something you'll regret, but it's still rude).

**Learn when you need a cooling-off period.** If you are tempted to respond out of anger, don't do it! Wait until your head is clear again. Learn how long you need to cool off. Some people only need an hour. Others should sleep on it. Still, others require several days. Whatever you do, don't send that angry e-mail or post to social media *until* you've had adequate time to cool off. And it's not just anger that clouds our judgment. Sometimes people make desperate, impulsive choices out of fear or sadness (e.g., quitting one job and moving to another without carefully thinking it through). The key here is to figure out how much time you need to gain back your self-control. Then take the time you need.

**Finally, try your best to get to the root of the things that tend to threaten your self-control.** What are they, and why are you so sensitive to them? A clue is to notice when your response is disproportionate to the offense—what many would call an overreaction. When this happens, it usually means there is something else that is the real problem beyond the immediate problem. For example, if someone in your office brings everyone coffee but you, then you would understandably be a little disappointed. But the same circumstance can make you seethe with anger if you struggle with overwhelming feelings of being rejected by others all your life. In this case, the real issue is not that your office mate didn't bring you coffee. The real root issue is that you (probably subconsciously) felt that this oversight was another example of the rejection you feel you have suffered from others. That pain of rejection hurt you, and the hurt turned to anger.

## *Learn to Recognize Pain*

It is important to learn how to *recognize* pain. Remember that one of the reasons people complain is because they are in pain. Most of us prefer to avoid pain, so we do all sorts of things to get away from it or make it go away. But many of these response behaviors are unhealthy and confusing to us and others. This is especially true if they or we do not understand the cause of our behavior. That is why learning to recognize pain is so important to the creation of a 'no complaining' organizational culture. Because when we can recognize pain, we can acknowledge it *as* pain and deal constructively with it.

So how do we recognize pain? It's not always as easy as we might think. An important part of learning to recognize pain is to understand that sadness, hurt, fear, and shame are forms of pain. Sometimes these things are obvious sources of pain, but other times they appear as symptoms that are harder to connect to pain.

**Sadness is typical pain and is often easier to recognize as pain.** For example, you might be grieving because a beloved colleague is leaving the organization, or maybe you experienced a tragedy at home. The sadness surrounding such circumstances is usually pretty obvious. You might feel disappointed because you didn't get a promotion, and that causes sadness. In a more severe form, you might experience the sadness that comes from feelings of hopelessness. Sadness hurts, and most of us can see that.

**Hurt and fear also cause pain, though sometimes people don't associate pain with these emotions.** When something hurts our feelings, we suffer pain. When we are afraid, we suffer a form of pain. The problem is that hurt and fear often do not appear as hurt and fear. That's because these emotions frequently turn into *anger* almost instantaneously. Consequently, we don't recognize them.

The problem with this is that anger is difficult to associate with pain. The key is to realize that anger is usually a *symptom* of pain. Since hurt often turns quickly to anger, it is hard to notice. Further complicating this is the fact that some people are more comfortable with anger than with hurt. This is particularly true of many men, but women experience it also. The result is that if someone says something mean to us, we might think we are angry, but we are really hurt—and that hurt has instantly turned to anger. Consequently, rather than deal with the pain of being hurt (which would address the real issue), we lash out in anger (which likely makes the situation worse).

Fear is similar in that it also can quickly turn to anger before we notice it as fear. For example, we might get angry at something that is making us afraid—a product delay. We might think we are just angry at the product delay itself. But fear turned to anger is the real reason we have boiled over. This is because—even though we might not realize it—we think that the product delay will lose a customer, which will affect our pay, which might make us unable to pay our mortgage, which might cost us our home! In other words, our intense anger is actually the fear of losing our home, and that fear is causing us a lot of pain. But rather than constructively address the pain of our fear, we unleash our anger on the product developers in ways that seriously harm our relationship with them.

**Shame is another emotion that is incredibly powerful and often very difficult to recognize.** Sometimes people confuse the feelings of shame and guilt, so let me clarify the difference with a helpful distinction. Guilt is feeling bad about something we've *done*—it can be productive when our conscience is correcting something that needs to be corrected. Shame is feeling bad about who we *are*—it is never productive. Fair treatment of shame requires a lot more discussion than I can address here, but I want to stress that shame is the source of enormous pain. Because the pain of shame is so intense, people do all sorts of things to avoid its sting.

Consequently, shame shows up in our lives in a variety of ways. For example, shame can make us exceedingly sensitive to certain self-doubts or to even the most sensitively conveyed constructive criticism. Shame can cause us to isolate ourselves from others because we feel that their gaze exposes our shame. We can put others down, either overtly or just in our minds, so that they don't threaten to aggravate our shame by making us feel unworthy or inferior. We can desperately chase after success and affirmation to cover up our shame, and we can get exceedingly angry if we don't get it. Those are just a few examples of how we can respond to shame in unhealthy ways.

Almost nobody completely escapes the effects of shame. But if you recognize that shame is particularly intense for you, I recommend that you seek assistance from someone who can help you understand its roots and learn to appreciate how much you matter for who you are as the *real* you—*not* for what you do or for any masks that you've learned to put on. The important thing, for now, is to try to recognize the pain of shame and the way it affects your feelings, thoughts, and behavior.

## *Deal with Sadness, Hurt, Fear, and Shame as Pain*

An effective way to deal with sadness, hurt, fear, and shame is to treat them as things that cause pain. You do this by first acknowledging that you are suffering pain and then taking positive, deliberate steps to manage that pain.

It's important to understand that acknowledging that you're suffering pain does not at all mean you are helpless, weak, or indulging in self-pity. Think about it. If you're suffering pain but don't admit it, then you're still suffering pain. That doesn't change. The pain most likely just shows up in unhealthy ways, like depression, anger, isolation, emotional coldness, hardening towards others' feelings, and so on.

When you acknowledge the pain, however, you're simply saying, "yes, that's painful (maybe *very* painful)—now, how can I address that pain constructively?" While there are specifics that can help with each of these forms of pain, here are some general practices that can help provide some relief:

- **Feeling heard**—just talking to another person who knows how to listen can be a great relief. This is not necessarily complaining if it is done deliberately for constructive healing (I'll address this more in Chapter Twelve on Peer Support)

- **Faith or something that gives you meaning**—many people find comfort in their faith tradition or in something that feels sublime to them. These things can help provide some meaning to your suffering and potentially some reassurance and hope.

- **Catching your breath and taking action**—if you need to take a walk, do it. If you need to sit and think, do it. If you need to weep, do it. These things are healthy practices that can release chemicals that help relieve pain. So, after you've grieved a while and caught your breath, go wash your face (so to speak), and figure out what's next. If another person hurt you, talk to the person, using the ground rules from Chapter Five.

- **Doing something fun**—you don't want to use fun activities as a cover that allows you to avoid facing your problems, but doing something healthy that you enjoy can boost your spirits. It sounds simple, but it can put you in a better mindset to think things through (see "Stop Ruminating and Start Reflecting" below). Can you identify activities that boost your spirits? If you can't identify any healthy activities that bring you joy, take a moment to identify some now. It's far easier to identify them when things are good than when your mind is clouded by pain.

- **Time**—if you address pain in healthy ways and take care of yourself, pain generally subsides over time. Be patient and persevere.

## *Recognize and Address Anxiety*

Fear is sometimes obvious and strong, like when you meet a snarling dog in the middle of the street. But for many of us, fear often shows up as a sort of low-level anxiety that can be harder to identify. This low-level anxiety can even cause symptoms that are not always obviously associated with anxiety. Here are several ways anxiety frequently appears in our lives:

- **Health issues**—anxiety and the stress that comes from it are behind an enormous number of health issues, like high blood pressure, high cholesterol, heart palpitations, headaches and other unexplainable pain, asthma, allergic reactions, diabetes, and others (though anxiety is not always the main cause of these conditions).

- **Distraction**—anxiety can make our minds feel muddled and confused. We can have trouble focusing and difficulty expressing our thoughts or ideas.

- **Impatience**—anxiety can make us generally irritable and less resilient to the normal roadblocks that we encounter every day, like a long line at the coffee house or a co-worker that is being difficult.

If you are experiencing any of these symptoms, consider the possibility that you might be anxious about something. One of the things that makes it difficult for people to recognize anxiety and its source is the tendency of anxious people to keep their minds (and often their bodies) moving constantly. This can be an unconscious way people cope with anxiety. The problem is that you most likely will need to slow yourself down to be able to discern the anxiety and its source.

The following process can be an important part of finding some relief from anxiety (note: in my experience, many people are familiar with this process, but few actually *practice* it with diligence):

- **STEP 1: Identify what is worrying you**—this is not always easy, so you'll have to slow down and be deliberate about exploring this question. It can help to process with a pen and paper and write down each thing that is worrying you. Often writing one will lead to the identification of others.

- **STEP 2: Address what you can change**—as you consider your list, highlight those items you think you can do something about. Then write down some specific steps you can take to address the issues. Prioritize the action steps and then do the first one as soon as you can (this will lead to the second and so on). You'll be surprised at how having a plan and working it will bring you some relief.

- **STEP 3: Accept what you can't change**—as you move through your list, prioritize, and make your action plan, you will identify some issues that you probably cannot change. The key here is to make peace with those things by acknowledging that they are what they are, and you will learn to live with them. As futile as it may seem, much anxiety comes from our refusal to accept things we can do nothing about, as if we think that refusing to accept such things will somehow change them. Faith traditions, spirituality, or positive personal life philosophies can help with this acceptance.

Family, friends, or trusted colleagues can be a great help in working through these steps (see Chapter Twelve on Peer Support). If your anxiety is especially debilitating, you might consider seeing someone who has some specific experience helping people with anxiety.

Before leaving this topic, let me point to a specific source of anxiety that I frequently see in the workplace—decision making. Most people face decisions from time to time. Sometimes those decisions seem especially difficult and agonizing with no easy and obvious options. Often our response is to put off the decision as long as we can. In the meantime, we are haunted by the anxiety of knowing that we will have to make the decision and wondering if we will make the right choice.

**Here is a process that can help when facing a difficult decision.** First, recognize that it is causing you anxiety. Next, determine how much time you have to consider the options. Take as much time as you can to educate yourself about the decision (include others in this process if appropriate). Then make a decision and own it! Don't make excuses. If it's your decision to make, then take responsibility for it. If it turns out it was the wrong decision (something every decision-maker has experienced at some time), admit it, correct it, and move on. Don't make this more emotionally complicated than it needs to be. The more decisions you practice making, the better you will become at it. And the less anxiety decision making will cause you.

## *Examine Yourself for Negativity*

An important source of complaining that we all must consider is our tendency toward negativity. Winston Churchill once defined a pessimist as someone who sees the difficulty in every opportunity and an optimist as someone who sees the opportunity in every difficulty. Sometimes we frame this as some people see a glass as half-full, and others see it as half-empty. Which of these do you tend towards?

I'm not suggesting we should have a naive optimism that is unable to see problems that must be addressed. But there is a difference between a sober-minded analysis that can identify positive and negative elements in a circumstance and habitual negativity that almost always chooses to wallow in the worst qualities of virtually everything.

The problem is that chronic negativity is more than just a personality quirk. There is considerable research showing how this kind of negativity affects mental and emotional health, physical health, and others who are in contact with the negative person. Chronic negativity and cynicism can impair your brain's cognitive functions and has even been associated with dementia. It can cause serious problems with your cardiovascular and immune systems. It actually rewires your brain to be more naturally negative, which makes it harder to be positive. And negativity spreads to those around you, impacting their health and productivity also.

**Therefore, we all must examine ourselves carefully for negativity.** I have found that an honest exploration of the following questions can help detect negativity:

- **Do I enjoy complaining?** This may seem silly, but the truth is that some of us really do enjoy complaining. To test this, try to go an entire day without saying one negative thing. If you enjoy complaining, you'll likely find that you become very uncomfortable holding it in.

- **Do I enjoy being angry at someone else?** Some people love to have an enemy—someone who 'deserves' their anger; someone who they can hate or despise in a way they can justify. Observe yourself carefully and consider who you complain about and why you are really complaining about those people.

- **Do I enjoy feeling like a victim?** Listen, if someone is treating you unjustly, then do something about it if you can. But try to be honest with yourself about whether you enjoy feeling like someone who has been victimized by another person, by a circumstance, or by life in general. Carefully consider how you would feel if the injustice you think you've experienced were completely gone. Would you truly be content, or would you look around for something else to replace it?

- **Do I have a bad attitude?** Consider whether you chronically see the glass as half empty. Observe yourself when presented with a challenge. Can you only see ways in which things can go bad? Or can you also spot the way forward? Ask yourself if you have become generally cynical and suspicious.

Be aware that negativity is very hard to change. But if you recognize that you are prone to negativity, you *must* work diligently to transform that negativity into something constructive—for your own sake.

**Here are a few practices that can help you deal with chronic negativity:**

- **Acknowledge your negativity**—the more precise and detailed the acknowledgment of your negativity is, the more success you will have at changing. Saying "sometimes I am negative" is good, but a more detailed acknowledgment like, "I really enjoy complaining and being angry at other people" is better.

- **Make a bold choice to change**—once you have acknowledged your negativity, be very specific and clearly declare that you will make changing and being more positive a priority. Remind yourself that you are taking responsibility and making a choice to change.

- **Recognize that being negative is bad for your health (and for those around you)**—reinforce your choice to change by understanding and reminding yourself of the consequences of your negativity.

- **Practice deliberate gratitude**—just as negativity has a negative effect on health, there is a lot of research showing how gratitude has a positive effect on health. Gratitude also helps rewire your brain to be more naturally positive. The key to gratitude is to be deliberate about it. Make a list of everything you are grateful for and spend some time reflecting on how grateful you are. If there is someone you can thank (e.g., another person, God, the universe), then express your thanks.

- **Pay attention to your body language**—most people don't realize how connected their body language is to their emotions, but this connection is significant. Negative people tend to scowl more, laugh less, and carry themselves more rigidly. This reinforces their internal negativity. To change this, make it a point to smile more, even when you don't feel like it. Laugh deliberately whenever you can, even if it starts as a small giggle. Soften your eyes by practicing smiling with your eyes. Loosen up your body when you feel yourself being rigid and stiff. You'll be surprised at how your emotions and thoughts begin to respond to these changes in your body language.

## Try Not to Hold a Grudge

There is considerable research showing that the ability to forgive is associated with good health. Conversely, holding a grudge and desiring revenge is harmful to our health. Therefore, we need to be honest about our propensity to hold a grudge. Here are some questions that can help you understand this better.

**Are you aware of your own tendency to hold a grudge when you perceive that someone has hurt you in some way?** Do you forgive easily? Or, do you punish people in some way (e.g., the silent treatment, making life difficult for them, cruelty, etc.) when they wrong you?

**Can you trace any of your motivations back to a desire to beat someone else in some way in order to "show them"?** How much of what you do is driven by this desire? Did you know that there are people who have committed their entire careers to somehow getting revenge?

**Do you enjoy holding a grudge?** Very few people would admit this, but I see it frequently. Hating feels good to some people. If they didn't have something to be angry at, they would invent it. So, ask yourself, "Do I enjoy being against something or outraged by it?" How much to I like to be able to blame someone else (a co-worker, a leader, a group of people) for my problems?

These strong feelings of resentment will affect our health, and they can also build up over time and cause us to do cruel things. Learning to forgive is difficult, but it is a critical skill to develop.

Here are some initial steps you can take when you feel that a person, a group of people, or an organization has committed an injustice against you:

- **STEP 1: Be honest with yourself**—take a careful look at your motivations. If you tend to harbor a grudge, acknowledge it. Consider why you are holding onto this grudge and be honest with yourself. It can help to talk this through with someone you trust who will be honest with you.

- **STEP 2: Acknowledge that the injustice as wrong and hurtful**—if you were treated unjustly, then acknowledge it. Forgiveness is not turning a blind eye toward injustice. It is important to acknowledge that what was done to you was wrong and that it caused you pain.

- **STEP 3: Go to the person to work things out (if possible)**— it is much easier to forgive someone when he or she has had an opportunity to apologize. Therefore, if the circumstances allow, try to go to the people who you think wronged you and explain to them how they hurt you. Be open to hear their side of the story and apologize to them if appropriate.

- **STEP 4: Determine whether you need to take remedial measures**—in some instances, you may not be able to work things out with the other party. Depending upon the nature of the violation, you might need to report the person to a supervisor, bring in a mediator, or take some form of legal action. Note that this is a practical step you've decided is appropriate. It should not be motivated by a desire for vengeance.

As you pursue the practical steps above, you will also need to address the strong emotions involved in the process of forgiveness. Forgiving can be challenging, so be patient with yourself. But don't give up. Harboring resentment and anger will chew you up from the inside out.

**Here are some steps that will help you handle the strong emotions associated with forgiveness:**

- **STEP 1: Empathize with the one who hurt you**—the more you can see the other person as a human being like you with flaws and challenges and pain, the easier it will be to forgive. Note that empathizing is not the same as excusing or justifying the person's actions.

- **STEP 2: Determine to let go of your desire for revenge**—this might involve ceasing any actual efforts you are making to hurt the perpetrator in some way, or just giving up your desire to see bad things happen to that person. It can be helpful to remind yourself that holding onto a desire for revenge will hurt you more than it will hurt the person who harmed you.

- **STEP 3: Be vigilant**—even if you work through these steps successfully and experience some unburdening from your desire for revenge, you will probably experience times when you feel anger and resentment building again. Be vigilant and watch for this. It's normal and understandable—forgiveness takes time. But when you notice it, be sure you repeat this process. It can be helpful to ask a friend to hold you accountable and check in with you periodically to see how you are doing with the process of forgiving.

## *Don't Chase the Wrong Things*

One of the sources of frustration and despair comes from chasing after the wrong things. When I say the "wrong things," I'm referring to things people *think* are most important to them, but that turn out *not* to be as important as they thought. Making this worse, these same people have often sacrificed the things that turn out to be truly important in order to pursue the wrong things.

**There are usually two general phases to chasing the wrong things:**

- **Phase one** is the period in which people are *not* aware they are chasing the wrong things. This phase is marked by frustration and restlessness.

- **Phase two** comes when people finally *realize* that they've been chasing after the wrong things. This phase is marked by despair, often accompanied by cynicism and anger.

The time frame for each of these periods varies for different people. Note that during phase two, people often make even more tragic and destructive choices than they did during phase one.

The key to avoiding the frustration of phase one and the despair of phase two is to try your best to understand your true priorities and to distinguish between your real values and those that masquerade as important. It is not always easy to tell the difference. But here are some serious questions you'll want to work through.

**Are you sacrificing your health or your family for money, power, or prestige?**

The allure of money, power, and prestige is easy for most of us to understand. The thought of having one (or all) of these things can create all sorts of temptation for us. In fact, this temptation can be so strong that we will find ways to justify sacrificing the things that should matter most, namely our health and our closest relationships.

It's not that money, power, and prestige are bad things to have. The problem is that when these temptations become the *most* important things to us, they become our primary objectives. That usually means we will viciously attack anything that stands in our way of getting them. It means we will even find ways to justify sacrificing our health and families to them.

### How susceptible to peer pressure are you?

Another thing that drives people to chase after the wrong things is peer pressure. Peer pressure is when our concern with what others think of us compels us to make choices and elevate priorities that are not in line with our true values. I have observed three organizational cultures that tend to generate this kind of peer pressure. Are you particularly susceptible to one of them?

- **Culture of "success"**—people pride themselves on putting in 80-hour weeks, being the first in the office and the last to leave, always being available by phone, answering e-mails during off-hours, and so on. They look down on anyone who falls short of these standards.

- **Culture of "toughness"**—people pride themselves on their ability to endure hardship without "whining" about it. People do not admit to areas of vulnerability or weakness, and they look down on anyone who does.

- **Culture of "sacrifice"**—people pride themselves on the sacrifices they make for the cause. Frazzled nerves and poor health are often seen as marks of honor. I find this especially prevalent in helping trades and non-profits.

Notice that each of these cultures involves the corruption of good things. Working hard and faithfully is a good thing; a culture of "success" is a corruption. Courageously overcoming adversity is a good thing; a culture of "toughness" is a corruption. Offering yourself generously to a worthy cause is a good thing; a culture of "sacrifice" is a corruption.

Overcoming this kind of peer pressure is difficult because most of us care a lot about what others think of us (though we try to fool ourselves into thinking we don't!). We can rarely avoid it entirely, but we can resist it. But doing so takes tremendous courage and honesty. You might start by being honest with yourself in thinking through these questions.

**Questions that can help you determine your susceptibility to peer pressure:**

- How aware are you of how much you're influenced by what others think?
- Do you need other people to get ahead?
- Do you need others to admire you?
- Do you need others to think you're tough or a hard worker?
- Can you look yourself in the mirror and honestly say that you are working hard?
- Do you know what lines you will not cross, no matter what it costs you?
- Can you make peace with the fact that you may give up something (e.g., money, power, prestige, approval, success, etc.) if you choose the most important things?

Let me clarify something. I'm not trying to tell you that working long hours and making certain sacrifices is right or wrong. Ultimately, you are the one who must live with your choices, and I certainly do think that having the integrity to be a dependable and hard-working employee should hold for everyone. I'm just trying to help you think through the *reasons* you are making those choices and help you recognize any *tradeoffs* you may be making (e.g., family for career).

The more you can honestly clarify the things that are most important to you, the better you will be able to make choices and sacrifices that are consistent with those values. When you do this well, you will be less likely to have a crisis in the future and less frustrated along the way.

## *Reflect Don't Ruminate*

An important part of developing self-awareness is being able to spend some time thinking deeply about how we feel and why we feel like we do; what we think and why we think what we think; what we do and why we do what we do. But there are healthy and unhealthy ways to do this deep work. There's an important distinction between reflection and rumination.

- **Reflection** is carefully and deliberately considering our feelings, behaviors, and motivations in order to deepen our understanding in ways that enable us to respond constructively in some way.

- **Rumination** is dwelling on unhealthy feelings or thoughts in ways that seem to be out of our control, are not productive, and have no purpose.

There is considerable research showing that *reflection is healthy*, whereas *rumination is harmful*. It can be helpful, therefore, to learn to tell the difference between reflection and rumination. Here are some questions that can help.

### Do I tend to see all the ways a situation can go bad?

Some people can think of 100 ways a situation can go wrong. They almost automatically rehearse *every* possibility in their minds, and it causes a lot of anxiety. The way to change this rumination into reflection is to realize that, most likely, only two or three of these possibilities are truly worth thinking about. When you narrow this list way down, you can constructively plan reasonable contingencies for each possibility that remains.

### Do I tend to go straight to the worst-case scenario?

This is like when you hear a news report that job growth for the month was not as vigorous as the previous month. Then your mind follows a path that asks one 'what if' question after another. What if the economy tanks? What if the organization lays me off? What if we lose the house? What if there's no room at the homeless shelter? And so on. The way to change this rumination into reflection is to recognize your tendency to do this, stop the progression, and laugh at yourself. Then reflect constructively about whether you truly need to take some action. You most likely do not.

### Am I replaying something in my mind?

One common form of rumination is when we replay in our minds a conversation we had with someone or a 'performance' we gave (e.g., giving a presentation). Sometimes we replay these things because of shame. We think we should have done or said something differently, and shame causes us to beat ourselves up or desperately recall something we did that makes it "not *so* bad." Other times we're angry about how a conversation went, but we feel helpless. So, we fantasize about a scenario in which we "put the person in his place" over and over. Both forms of rumination are harmful. Healthy reflection, on the other hand, will help you give yourself grace and learn from your less than perfect performance. It will help you think through whether you really need to revisit the conversation that went bad or just accept and forgive.

### Am I indulging in self-pity?

Self-pity seems to feel good, but it is rarely helpful or constructive. Ceasing the rumination of self-pity is very different from constructively reflecting on your suffering. Acknowledging your pain as suffering is an important part of addressing it in a healthy way (refer to "Dealing with Sadness, Hurt, Fear, and Shame" earlier in this chapter).

**Here are a few techniques that can help you engage in healthy, constructive reflection:**

- **Ask yourself whether your thinking is helpful**—learning from mistakes is helpful, but beating yourself up is not. Making a plan to address something you can change is helpful, but worrying about what you can't change is not. If you recognize that your thinking is not helpful, acknowledge that it just hurts you and make a choice to try not to dwell on it.

- **Ask yourself constructive questions,** like...
  ⇒ What emotions am I feeling?
  ⇒ What do I really want?
  ⇒ What is making me afraid?
  ⇒ What has hurt my feelings?
  ⇒ What is the root of my anger? Is it hurt, fear, shame, injustice, or something else?
  ⇒ Why am I allowing other people to define what I think of myself?

- **Think this through with a trusted listener**—bear in mind that speaking with another person is not complaining when your goal is constructive reflection. Research shows that *ruminating* together is harmful (that is what complaining is), but *reflecting* together is helpful.

Constructive reflecting is essential to growing in self-awareness, problem-solving, and recovering from emotional challenges. Learn how to do it well. Destructive rumination accomplishes nothing and only harms you. Try your best to avoid it.

## *Evaluate Your Interpersonal Communications Skills*

As you are learning to self-reflect, you should also honestly assess how you are doing with the interpersonal communications techniques we discussed in Chapters Five and Six. I recommend that you refer to that chapter for specifics, but here are some questions to consider that are based upon the ideas found there. As you work through this list, identify the questions that you think you do pretty well (this will encourage you) and also identify those you need to work on (this will guide you).

**Interpersonal skills evaluation questions:**

- Am I willing to engage in uncomfortable conversations, or do I tend to run from them?
- Which communication ground rules do I do naturally, and which do I need to work on? Why do I think that is?
- How empathetic am I? Does empathy come naturally for me?
- How well can I describe my thoughts and feelings? Am I willing to do that with others when appropriate?
- How likely am I to accuse someone of something rather than ask?
- Do I tend to trust people? Why or why not? Do I tend to suspect their motivations (e.g., if they don't say hello or return a call or email or text?)
- Do I know how to be productively honest? How often do I practice this?
- How often do I show respect to others? Do I only respect my superiors? Or do I respect everyone?
- What kind of conflict style do I usually employ? Do I understand how my conflict style interacts with other conflict styles?
- How well do I think I listen to others? Was I aware that listening was a skill to be developed? How important do I think listening is and why?
- Do I tend to get defensive? If so, why?
- Am I ever mean to others? Why do I think this is?
- Do I have hesitancy about using these ground rules? Why or why not?
- Have I ever seriously reflected on my attitude about vertical respect (i.e., respect for my leaders or respect for my subordinates)?
- What do I think of leaders in general?
- What kind of leader do I prefer?
- What kind of leader am I, and how do I tend to communicate?
- Am I a secure or anxious leader? (i.e., Am I worried about impressing others? Am I always trying to get credit? Do I always interrupt?)

## *Learn Relaxation and Reflection Techniques*

An important part of self-awareness is learning how to manage our emotions. We all have emotions, and this is a good thing—without them, we would just be living computers. But emotions can be challenging. Sometimes our emotional responses affect some very deep parts of our brains, and this impacts our bodies. An example of this is when we have a difficult conversation with someone and find that our hands are shaking after we get back to our desk.

One of the most effective practices for rewiring our deep brain is relaxation and reflection techniques. You might hear this referred to as meditation, contemplative prayer, or mindfulness. Unfortunately, despite the effectiveness of these methods, they are seriously underutilized.

In teaching these techniques, I have found that there are generally two kinds of people—doers and reflectors. Doers don't like to reflect, and reflectors can be reluctant to do. What this means in practice is that it's exceedingly difficult to get doers to sit still long enough to practice these techniques. Reflectors, on the other hand, are more willing to sit still. But they can be reluctant to follow any sort of structured approach to relaxation, and they can sometimes want to remain in a reflective state in order to avoid taking helpful actions.

Do you tend to be more of a doer or a reflector? Whichever you are, I want to encourage you to learn and practice the technique I am going to describe. This will help you manage your emotions, clear your mind, reduce stress, and generally improve your health. The more easily you can get in and out of a relaxed state, the more easily you'll be able to do so in stressful times. Spending just a few minutes each day with this technique can familiarize your mind and body with deep relaxation. This will help you even if you are a highly extroverted, high energy person.

There are several approaches to reflection and relaxation. I have distilled a few of the most important elements, and you can adapt them to your own spiritual or health practices.

**Elements of reflection and relaxation:**

- **Use a timer**—a key practice is to set a timer (this is especially important for beginners!). Start with just five minutes. Almost anyone can sit still for five minutes. After a few days, increase it to seven minutes. Try to work up to ten minutes (or more if you'd like). At the end of the timer, if you feel like you are not ready to stop, then continue the technique for as long as you want to continue.

- **Follow these simple steps:**
  ⇒ **Breathing**—focus on slowing down your breath for a few minutes. It can help to breathe in through your nose and out through your mouth. Feel the breath going deep down into your belly.
  ⇒ **Sense your body**—after you've focused on your breath, begin to work through every part of your body. Just try to become aware of those parts. For example, you might focus on your toes (wiggling them helps you feel them) and then the bottoms of your feet on up through the rest of your body.
  ⇒ **Self-reflect**—gently notice the emotions that you are feeling. Ask yourself, "What is the emotion I'm feeling? Why am I feeling it?"

- **Use Prayer or Meditation**—if you have a certain faith or spirituality, you can reflect on God or whatever belief that is appropriate for you. If you don't have a spiritual belief, reflecting on something profound (e.g., the size of the universe, the depth of the ocean, the vastness of a mountain, etc.) can be helpful.

Keep in mind that this technique takes practice, and it takes time to see the benefits. If you do this in a disciplined way for at least ten minutes each day, at least five days per week for three months, I am confident that you will see progress. Give it a try!

## Care for Your Body

Your mind, emotions, and body are all interconnected (and spirit if you believe that). The health of each affects the health of the others. Nevertheless, my observation is that many people do not pay much attention to this interconnection.

This disconnect is especially true when people have some type of emotional challenge. In my observation, these people often seek emotional solutions and ignore their bodies. The problem with this is that the state of our bodies affects the state of our mind and emotions. The simple solution is—take care of your body.

Honestly, caring for your body is usually pretty simple. The problem is execution. We just don't *do* it. So, I'm going to give you a brief list of things that will help you care for your body. This is nothing you haven't heard before. But hopefully, it will serve as a reminder. Again, the point here is that this is important! So, look over this list and identify what you do well and what you need to improve.

**Basic care of your body:**

- **Drink plenty of water**—being well hydrated is important for your organs and other body parts to function well. Also, when you get dehydrated, you'll be less resilient to anxiety, so you'll be more irritable, distracted, and fog-brained. And you'll have less energy. So, take deliberate steps to stay hydrated. Many people get so busy that they *forget* to drink water. Carry around a water bottle if you need to. And drink pure water. I'm not saying that you should never drink anything other than water. But use other drinks as an occasional treat. Don't use them to hydrate.

- **Eat well**—what you feed your body matters, so eat a good diet of healthy food. Everyone is a little different, so you may ask a doctor or nutritionist what the best diet for your body type and metabolism should be. Avoid eating lots of processed junk food. Figure out what foods give you energy and clarity of mind. If you get irritable when you are hungry, then you can bet that your diet and your emotional state is strongly connected. Figure out what you need to do to keep yourself well-nourished during the day.

- **Get some exercise**—you should find time for regular exercise like running, biking, aerobics class, or something like that. At a minimum, stay active and move your body. Get your heart rate up at least a little bit during the day. A stagnant lifestyle is a major contributor to health problems. If you have a job where you must sit for long periods, set a timer for 30 minutes intervals, and get up and move and stretch for a minute or two every time it goes off.

- **Get plenty of sleep**—everyone is different. Some people seem to need more sleep than others. But sleep is critical for your mind, body, and emotions to be healthy. When people skimp on sleep, they impair their cognitive functions, their body's ability to heal, and their emotional stability. So, make sleep a priority.

- **Get regular wellness checks**—it's better to be proactive about seeing your doctor than it is to only visit when you're sick. The doctor can hopefully find problems before they get too serious and can offer specific recommendations about hydration, sleep, exercise, and diet. When was the last time you had a wellness check? Put it in your calendar as a recurring activity and make it happen. Think about it—if you ignore your physical health *until* you have a crisis, you will be far less productive while you are trying to recover.

## Give Yourself Grace

I'll end this section with encouragement and caution. As you start to self-reflect, sometimes you see things you don't like very much. When we see unpleasant things about ourselves, a common response is to look away as fast as we can, make excuses and justifications, or collapse in a corner somewhere. None of these responses is productive.

When you notice unflattering things about yourself, the first thing to do is relax—don't panic, it will be fine. Give yourself grace. Everyone has areas where they can grow. And, if I may be a little more direct, we all have qualities that are a little bit ugly. The only difference is that some people are aware of these things, and others are not.

Therefore, when you unearth one of these not so pleasant elements of your personality, celebrate. Yes, I mean celebrate. Please believe me when I say that people who are oblivious to their blind spots are more common that those who have the courage and acumen to find and face them honestly.

So, if you discover a blind spot, celebrate! What you have done is discovered an opportunity for change. That is really what these unpleasant things are. So, think of them as opportunities for change, not things that determine your value.

Psychologist Carol Dweck's popular book *Mindset* is helpful here. Her research identified two general attitudes about self-development that she called a 'fixed mindset' and a 'growth mindset.' People with a fixed mindset did not believe they could change. Therefore, anything that pointed out their shortcomings was just bad news because they believed nothing could be done about them. On the other hand, people with a growth mindset were confident that they *could* change. Those people welcomed constructive critique because it helped them identify areas for growth.

Nevertheless, people entering a serious self-awareness process for the first time can become very disoriented for a while. It can start to feel like you're learning to walk again. It can erode your confidence. That's okay. It's normal. It happens to everyone. It's not forever. Eventually, you will begin to gain back your confidence as you develop new skills and get better at utilizing them. So, don't get discouraged. Think of yourself in a cocoon for a while. You'll emerge transformed.

# Practical Next Steps

As I wrap up this section, I want to provide a few practical next steps your organization can take to create a culture of self-awareness.

## Set an Example at the Top

In any organization, you'll have a *few* people who are interested in self-awareness. But the real benefit comes when *most* people in the organization are participating in the same self-awareness process and have made the same commitments. Self-awareness is uncomfortable and frightening for many people, so knowing that everyone is pursuing it can be reassuring.

To get the entire organization united in this effort, however, top leadership must pave the way. The head of the organization should acknowledge the importance of self-awareness for the individual health of every employee and for their effectiveness working together to execute the organization's mission. It is also critical that the head of the organization set an example by opening himself or herself up to a 360 review, an executive coach, or some other deliberate self-awareness process. The leader can then share some appropriate disclosure about what he or she has learned.

## Offer Formal Self-Awareness Training

It's not enough to merely explain the importance of self-awareness without also offering employees a tangible next step. It is important, therefore, to offer employees some formal self-awareness training. A good start is to teach the principles for creating a 'no complaining' culture found in this book. The human resources or learning and development departments might conduct the training. Or, you can bring in an outside consultant to do it. You can supplement this with other self-awareness inventories (e.g., such as DISC or MBTI). When I do workplace culture training, I use my own self-awareness process that I have found especially useful for effective team functioning. In any case, be sure you have a formal next step that employees can take.

## *Establish Peer Support*

An important component of self-awareness development is the opportunity for people to work with others who have some training to help them. Therefore, I strongly recommend that your organization create a peer support program. People trained to do peer support will be better able to help each other grow, hold each other accountable for complaining, resolve problems, and deal with unresolvable disappointments. The next chapter describes how to set this up.

# Questions for Reflection and Discussion

1. How can self-reflection help to address complaining?

2. Do you think self-awareness is important? Why or why not? Why do you think some people ignore self-reflection?

3. What is the difference between the inside person and the outside person? Are you more aware of the outside person or the inside person? Do you think your friends would agree with your answer?

4. What is the difference between self-knowledge and self-reflection?

5. Have you ever done any self-awareness work in the past? If so, what did you learn?

6. What are some key things you must practice in order to experience real transformation?

7. Which self-awareness techniques do you think you do well? Which do you need to work on? Why?

8. Why is it important to give yourself grace?

# CHAPTER TWELVE

# Establish Peer Support

The goal of this book is to help you create a 'no complaining' organizational culture. That means we want to effect long term change. For long term change to occur, it's important to have mechanisms in place that will *continue* to make a positive impact. Establishing a peer support structure will be a vital part of this enduring transformation.

## What is Peer Support?

**Peer support is non-professional helpers in the organization providing emotional and practical support to one another.**

These helpers could be anyone in the organization at any level, but they are probably *not* employed by the organization specifically to be a professional counselor (e.g., psychologists, counselors, chaplains, etc.) to the employees. The organization might employ such people (and these people would have an important role in a peer support system), but peer support is primarily dependent upon non-professional helpers.

If you think about it, many people in organizations engage in a form of peer support anyway. After all, complaining to a co-worker is a form of peer support. But we want to make this kind of peer support is deliberate and constructive, rather than undirected and destructive. We want to create a system of peer supporters who are trained to recognize complaining and to respond in ways that will help others resolve problems, address immediate frustrations, or endure unresolvable disappointments.

Peer support can be a formal or informal system. A formal peer support system has designated peer supporters, formal mechanisms to seek peer support, a formal peer support structure, and so on. An informal peer support system is where everyone in the organization is equipped with some basic peer support skills and encouraged to make their informal interactions with one another more constructive. Later in the chapter, I'll discuss which option might be best for your organization.

I want to be careful here and emphasize that what I'm describing in this book is peer support. I distinguish this from peer counselors. When I train peer counselors, I have higher expectations, and therefore I require a higher degree of training. While a peer support program could eventually graduate to peer counseling, the goal of this book is to provide organizations with relatively modest, achievable goals that will nevertheless make a substantive positive impact on everyone.

## Why is Peer Support Helpful?

It takes some work and commitment to implement a peer support program, so I'll take a moment to provide a few reasons why peer support is worth the effort.

### Work-Life and Home-Life are Connected

It used to be that employees were expected to be 'professionals' in the workplace. Often what people meant is that employees should not bring their personal problems to the office. I have had the opportunity to work in a variety of business settings and to lead churches as a pastor. This has given me the opportunity to observe the realities of employee personal lives and what this looks like in the workplace. I can tell you that people do not leave their problems at home.

In reality, problems at home most certainly affect performance in the workplace—perhaps a reduction in productivity, absenteeism, isolation from co-workers, irritability, and so on. Likewise, people do not leave their work problems at work. They bring them home and often take them out on their family and friends.

Most employed people spend over one-third of their waking hours at work (or working remotely). Not only is it difficult for employees to separate work and home life (as much as they might try to fake it), but these days younger generations want to be more authentic at work and reduce that separation. These younger people don't like the idea of being a 'professional' that puts on a mask at work, does the job, and goes home. This means that people are becoming more transparent at work about who they are—passions, dreams…and problems.

## Unproductive Dumping Saps Productivity

As a result of this trend to reduce the separation between home life and work life, employees are increasingly looking to people at work for support with all areas of life. Some research suggests that employees frequently turn to supervisors for this support, especially if they feel that their supervisor cares. (By the way, younger people especially are expressing that this is the kind of boss they want).

The problem is that when people dump their problems on their supervisor, she is often in a distracted mood for the rest of the day, which undermines her productivity. This is partially because many supervisors (especially those with less experience) don't feel they have the skill set to handle employee personal problems and partly because they think they're on their own in shouldering their employee's burdens.

Peer support can help with this because it provides training that gives supporters the confidence that they really can help co-workers in constructive ways. It also establishes a framework that the one seeking help and the peer supporter can use to transform unproductive dumping into constructive interaction. Finally, peer support creates a network of others who are also capable of providing support, and this reassures those providing the initial help that they are alone.

## Peer Support is Effective

Professional mental health workers play a vital role in helping people handle the challenges that life brings. But professional mental health is expensive, not always available, and often unnecessary. Many of the problems people deal with in the workplace don't need the specialization of a professional mental health worker. Even when a person is struggling with a more serious mental health problem and regularly sees a professional, that person can also benefit from the encouragement and concern shown by a peer supporter.

There are a variety of approaches to peer support, and there is a substantial amount of research evaluating the effectiveness of these programs. Overwhelmingly, the studies show that peer support provides significant improvements in quality of life to those people receiving it. Peer support also is beneficial to organizations because it reduces employee absenteeism and turnover, and it increases productivity and hiring effectiveness.

## Peer Support Can Give People Meaning

Many people want to have a sense that they are doing something significant with their lives and making a difference. This desire often becomes more pronounced when people get to middle age and begin to reflect on the legacy they will leave. Sociologists have also noted this desire in the younger generations of today. Certainly, one of the places people look for significance is in their work. But not all work feels significant. Consequently, some people hop from one job to another seeking significance.

Being a peer supporter can provide people with a sense of significance and a more positive feeling about their organization. Peer support helps employees focus on the *people* in the organization. This naturally creates an increased sense of commitment to the organization itself. Peer support can also provide meaning to employees who feel their job is mundane. The actual work task might not feel particularly significant, but the peer support mission gives new purpose to their employment.

# In Session Peer Support Techniques

This section provides a guide that the peer supporter can follow during a peer support session (whether this is a formal or informal session). The phases are as follows:

- Listen with patience
- Acknowledge with compassion
- Get information
- Help the person reflect
- Guide the person to action
- Follow up

The length of each of these phases will vary with the situation and could range from less than a minute to an hour or more.

## *PHASE 1—Listen with Patience*

When a person comes to you with a spontaneous peer support need or a planned peer support session, the first thing you'll want to do is **assess the urgency of the situation and de-escalate if necessary**. If the person is animated and upset, tell him it's okay if he needs to take a moment to calm down.

If you feel that you, the person, or anyone else is in **immediate danger** (either from the risk of violence or a health concern), **call 911** immediately.

**Allow the person to vent.** During this phase, resist the temptation to respond with a solution or interrupt. Until the person feels heard and calms down, he will not be able to process possible solutions anyhow.

**Stay fully engaged and focused on the person.** Avoid looking around the room, at your phone, at your watch, etc. This takes discipline, so practice.

**Simply listening to another person express himself can be incredibly powerful.** Don't underestimate the value of this. Remembering this will help you to listen without interrupting. (Obviously, if you feel you need to interrupt to assess whether there is an emergency, use common sense judgment).

## PHASE 2—Acknowledge with Compassion

**The best way to show compassion is to sincerely *feel* compassion.** It helps to take a moment to deliberately focus on the person's humanity by reflecting on the fact that she feels deeply, has dreams, has fears, has family, and so on.

Do your best to **empathize with the person** by imagining how you would feel if you were in the same circumstance.

**Remind yourself that this person is a work in progress.** Try to see her potential, rather than focusing on her flaws.

**Engage what the person is saying** with short, simple phrases that acknowledge her feelings, like "I'm sorry," "that sounds hard," "I'm listening," "yeah," "uh-huh."

Continue to **avoid the temptation to give advice or problem solve**. The *primary goal of this phase* (especially with a new person) is to get her to trust you, feel comfortable with you, and believe that you sincerely care.

## PHASE 3—Get Information

When you think the person has had an opportunity to share his concerns, you will want to begin to gather some information. Use your best judgment about what to ask, but here are some things to consider.

If you think the person just needs to vent one time, and it's not a particularly serious issue, then you can proceed to "Phase 4—Help the Person Reflect."

But, if the person is talking about a longer-term issue (such as chronic anxiety or depression), then **ask who is on his care team?** Any mental health professionals or clergy? Any other peer supporters in the organization? If the person does not have anyone else, consider encouraging him to involve others, especially if the issue seems serious.

If you suspect an immediate threat of some sort, then ask: **Are you having a physical health emergency? Are you thinking of killing yourself?** It's better to ask these questions than ignore them with disastrous consequences.

**Assess your timing.** Consider how long you think this session will take? How urgent is the situation? Is it okay to postpone if that is more convenient?

If it is a true emergency, it's important to address it right away. If you are not able to help for some reason, **get another peer support person involved.**

If you think it will be quick and you have the time, you might deal with it right at that moment. But, if it seems to require more time and you determine that it's not urgent, plan a time when you and the person you're supporting can revisit it. Get it on the calendar before you close the session.

## PHASE 4—Help the Person Reflect

**Ask helpful questions like:** What emotions are you feeling? Why do you think that? Is that thought helpful? Refer to the previous chapter on Self-reflection (e.g., if the person is struggling with negativity, help him work through the section "Examine Yourself for Negativity").

**Provide gentle accountability and correction.** Remember that you don't want to criticize complaining but rather treat it as a symptom to diagnose and heal.

**Don't condemn.** You will rarely make progress with a person by being judgmental and severe. She will just shut down and distance herself from you. Tough love should only be a last resort after you've earned the right to correct a little more directly. Also, remember that we are talking about techniques for a peer support scenario. This is not necessarily applicable to a normal job setting that may require tougher correctives in some circumstances.

**Remind the person that some things are "understandable but not helpful."** This is a good peer support technique when a gentle correction is needed, and it will help you speak truth with graciousness in a nonjudgmental way. For example, if a person is indulging in self-pity or if she lost her temper and said something regretful to someone, you can say, "that is understandable, but it's probably not helpful." This is a disarming way to correct without condemning.

**Be patient with people who are struggling to forgive.** Forgiveness is hard and takes time. Don't make the mistake of moralizing to a person who is having trouble forgiving. Don't say, "you know you're supposed to forgive!" Remind the person that forgiveness is a process. Again, you might say something like, "harboring that bitterness is understandable, but it's not helpful to you."

Celebrate breakthroughs when people make progress. Recognizing and acknowledging a character flaw is making progress. So congratulate, encourage, and accept the person when that happens. This alone will be amazingly helpful and reassuring.

## PHASE 5—Guide the Person to Action

Apply the 'no complaining' culture framework from Chapter Four to the issue:

**ALERT→APPLY (filter)→ACT**

**Identify why the complaining is happening.**

**Determine the reason for the complaining and the appropriate solution:**

- IF I am feeling helpless → THEN use Honoring Honesty to share my concerns with the appropriate people

- IF I am feeling frustrated by a problem → THEN employ the process of Problem Naming and Problem Solving

- IF I am in pain → THEN use Peer Support and Self-Awareness to pursue comfort, acceptance, and coping

- IF I have a bad attitude → THEN then use Peer Support and Self-Awareness to pursue growth and accountability

**Identify what practical steps the person should take next and utilize the other sections of the book as appropriate.** Determine if the person should: Refer to a peer support supervisor, a mental health professional, or another resource? Apologize to someone? Work a problem (use Chapters Eight, Nine, or Ten as a reference)? Take a walk? Explore an area of self-awareness (use Chapter Eleven as a reference)? Go back to work? Go to lunch? Go home? Some other constructive step?

**Write this next step on a notecard that the person can take with him.**

## PHASE 6—Follow Up

Before you close the peer support session, it is important to **determine when you will follow up**. Get it on the calendar before you dismiss.

If the issue isn't serious enough to need a formal follow up session, simply make a note to yourself to check in with the person in a week or so. Then, make a quick personal visit or send an e-mail or text and just say, "I just wanted to check in and see how things are going." Again, just having someone who cares will really mean a lot to most people, so don't underestimate the value of a simple 'touching base' sort of gesture. It matters!

# Principles to Follow

The in-session peer support techniques form a set of steps you can follow in an actual peer support session. But here are a few additional ideas and principles that will help you to be a more effective peer supporter.

## *Develop Your Self-awareness*

One of the most important things you can do to be a better peer supporter is to develop your self-awareness. The better you become at practicing the self-awareness techniques, the more effective you'll be at helping others. So, work on them diligently and deliberately.

## *Refer When Necessary*

Pride can make peer supporters reluctant to get help when they need it. Remember that you can't help everyone—or at least not you alone. Sometimes the person you are trying to help won't connect with you for some reason. That's okay. Help find another peer supporter she will connect with.

Sometimes you need help from someone else with different experience and expertise. So, you need to know what referral resources you have available. This might be higher-level peer support people, a corporate coach/chaplain, an outside professional of some sort (e.g., mental health, financial, marriage, medical, etc.), or a non-peer support supervisor if necessary.

At the same time, you don't want to punt. Fear can cause people to refer when they don't need to because they are sufficiently equipped to handle the situation. Just use your best judgment to determine what you should do.

## Don't Ever Recommend Discontinuation of Medication

Do not ever recommend that a person discontinue any medications he or she is taking. This could create a dangerous problem for the person and a serious liability for you as a peer supporter and for your organization.

Sometimes people in peer support situations will mention medications that they are taking. They might even express a desire to discontinue those medications. This may or may not be a good option for them, but it is *not* a question that you, as a peer supporter, should weigh in on. Do not ever give a recommendation about this, one way or another. Rather, acknowledge that this is a very important question and encourage the person to discuss it with his or her prescribing physician.

## Don't Accept Money

Sometimes if you help someone, they will offer you money—maybe as a gift, maybe as a tip, maybe because they think the peer supporter expects it. Whatever the reason, don't ever accept money for peer support activities. Accepting money for peer support activities should be against organizational policy. It also will corrupt the relationship you have with the person you are helping. Just don't do it.

Sometimes people will want to give you a small (non-monetary) gift to say thank you. I think that accepting a card, some flowers, an inexpensive trinket, or something like that is fine (though you should get this policy from your leadership). You certainly don't want to give the impression that you expect a gift—and in your mind, don't expect anything. But sometimes people want to say thank you with a small gift, and it is meaningful to them that you accept their gesture of appreciation.

## *Pay Attention to Power Differentials*

If you are a person's supervisor, it is generally not a good idea to do intense, on-going peer support with that person. It can put you and the person you're supporting in an awkward position. You may still get involved in some way, however. For example, the person getting help may need a change in work schedule. He may need your general support of the situation. Or, he may need your problem-solving ability.

## *Don't Make Hard Choices for People*

People will often ask you what you think they should do. What they really want is for you to decide *for* them. Don't do it! Your objective should be to help them think it through but don't decide for them. They are the ones who must live with their decision—not you. If you decide for them, they may resent you for it if they come to believe it was the wrong decision. Explain this to the person you are supporting.

Let me qualify here that I'm not talking about common sense recommendations or next steps when someone isn't thinking clearly. This kind of counsel can be very helpful. Rather, I am referring to big life decisions (e.g., whether to look for a new job, whether to seek a marital separation, etc.). Help the person think through this type of major decision, but don't make it for her.

## *Don't Allow Peer Support to Become Gossip*

People should become peer supporters because they truly want to help other people, not because they enjoy being nosy and hearing gossip about people's lives. As a peer supporter, be sure you respect the confidentiality of the person getting help. Ask if there are others who already know about the issue. If you think you should get other people involved (e.g., a supervisor, another peer supporter), ask the person for permission. Obviously, if you genuinely believe someone's life is in immediate jeopardy, you may have to bring in other appropriate parties even without the person's permission. Use your best judgment and approach this with common sense and respect.

Peer supporters must also ensure that the peer support session does not become a gossip session about another co-worker. Keep the conversion constructive. If you discuss a co-worker, be sure you are identifying next steps, which might include a meeting with that co-worker to work through a problem. Simply badmouthing someone with no constructive purpose is gossip, not peer support.

## *Watch Your Time*

If you are part of the peer support team, remember that you still have a job that you are paid to do. So, assess the seriousness and urgency of the issue and respond accordingly. Drop everything for emergencies and get appropriate people involved if necessary. Put off non-emergencies after about ten minutes and find a more appropriate time to follow up.

Be certain you are familiar with the peer support time guidelines your organization has approved and work within those guidelines. Monitor and record the time you're spending doing peer support. Indicate whether the session is during work time or off time (e.g., on a lunch break or after work).

## *Watch Your Emotional and Physical Health*

Take responsibility for keeping yourself emotionally and physically resilient. Peer supporters can only take so much, and sharing the burdens of others is draining. Watch yourself. Caring is a team sport. It's too much for one person. Going it alone results in burnout, and that doesn't help anyone.

So, don't take on more than you can handle. Get others involved as appropriate. If you are in a bad place emotionally, tell the peer support coordinator or refer people who come to you for support to others. It's better to wait until you are feeling more resilient than it is to jeopardize your health. You must approach this responsibly.

## You are Not Responsible "for" People, Rather You Are Responsible "to" People

What's the difference? It's the old saying, "You can lead a horse to water, but you can't make him drink." In other words, you can take responsibility for doing your best to advise and support a person, but you cannot shoulder the responsibility for the outcome—that is too much burden. Remembering this guideline will be a lifesaver as you encounter the challenges of trying to help people bear their burdens. So, memorize it and remind yourself often.

## Don't Give Away What You're Not Willing to Give Away

People who are in pain will often lean heavily on you. Sometimes their pain clouds their judgment such that they will take advantage of your charity. That's especially true as you become a more skilled and compassionate peer supporter because more people will be drawn to you for help. This is a good sign, but you need to manage it very carefully.

Caring people often don't know how to say "no" to hurting people. They give and give until they become resentful. Let me be very direct here. What you need to understand is that if you become resentful, it's your fault. That is why it's critical to follow this principle: Don't give away what you're not willing to give away.

When we give away something with the expectation of getting something in return, we are not truly giving—we're selling. In other words, there are strings attached to our gift. Therefore, if we don't get something back (e.g., gratitude, praise, a favor, etc.), we feel cheated and grow resentful.

Likewise, if someone asks us for something that we are not willing to give but we give it anyway, we are likely to grow resentful because we weren't willing to give it in the first place.

Therefore, before you give a significant amount of your time, advice, emotional energy, or anything else, make very certain that you are truly willing to give it away—with no strings attached, no expectations. *You* must take responsibility for this because nobody else will.

## *Express Specific Appreciation*

It's important to encourage people who receive peer support to express their gratitude to the people who helped them. This expression of gratitude is even more meaningful when the person can recount a few specific ways in which the peer supporter helped.

There is research showing how this kind of acknowledgment significantly encourages and energizes the peer supporter. When this acknowledgment of help is not given, however, the peer supporter is generally more anxious about whether he was helpful, how the person is doing now, and whether he should take some further action to help. So express appreciation to a peer supporter who helps you.

# Practical Next Steps

To help you establish peer support in your organization, here is a list of things to do to establish a peer support structure.

## *Decide the Type of Peer Support Structure You'll Use*

The first thing you'll need to do is decide whether you want to implement a formal, informal, or hybrid peer support structure. Here are some things to help you think that through.

An **informal structure** involves exposing all employees to the principles discussed in this book and encouraging everyone to be better supporters of one another. Nobody is specifically designated as a peer supporter. This can be helpful in smaller organizations of less than 25 people.

A **formal structure** is where certain people are designated, trained, and organized as peer supporters. This is generally necessary for larger organizations of more than 25 people.

A **hybrid structure** is ideal because there are some designated peer supporters with specific advanced training and experience (maybe overseen by a coach, chaplain, or counseling professional). Still, everyone in the organization receives at least the basic training found in this book.

## *Recruit and Train a Peer Support Team*

If you decide to implement a formal or hybrid peer support structure, you'll need to recruit peer supporters.

**A good peer supporter should have these qualities:**

- **Concern for people**—peer supporters should have a genuine concern for people. Note that this type of concern is not limited to a single personality type.

- **Maturity**—this does necessarily mean maturity in age, but rather a certain amount of wisdom and ability to respond well to difficult situations.

- **Current stability**—it's best that the peer supporter is in a place of relative emotional stability, not currently facing any major life stressors.

- **Responsible**—those turning to peer supporters for help are often in a place of vulnerability. Therefore, peer supporters must be the kind of people that can responsibly handle that vulnerability, be discreet, follow up, etc.

- **Committed**—peer supporters must be able to make a year commitment. It's best to screen out people who get excited about peer support, but then quickly lose interest.

- **Experienced in suffering**—this quality is not essential, but those who have experienced hardship and landed on their feet can often empathize well with others.

## Select peer supporters:

- Make organization-wide communications about the peer support program. Emphasize the importance of peer support and what peer supporters should expect. (see Appendix B for a sample communication template).

- Hold an information session for interested people

- Have the interested people complete an application form (see sample application in Appendix C)

## Train peer supporters:

- Schedule formal training

- Teach the techniques in this book

- Do some role-play regarding scenarios you anticipate peer supporters will encounter. This will build confidence among your peer supporters.

- You will want to plan quarterly training sessions for peer supporters. Two hours is usually adequate for follow-ups. Be sure to allow time for peer supporters to ask questions of more experienced people.

## *Consider Getting Specialized Help*

Creating a peer support team can go faster and smoother with the help of people who have experience training peer supporters. My firm, Remedium Solutions, can certainly provide this help, and there are others with this type of experience.

## Consider Employing Workplace Chaplains or Coaches

When establishing a peer support program, it can be helpful to have someone available who can oversee the program and serve as an escalation resource. Some organizations are large enough to have a staff counselor or psychologist. For others, a workplace chaplain or coach that makes regular visits to the organization can be a great part-time alternative.

## Determine Time Management Parameters

It's important that leaders permit peer supporters to take time to do peer support. That means the organization's leadership will have to answer the following questions clearly:

- How much time are peer supporters allowed to spend each week engaging in peer support activities?

- What is the preferred time of day that peer supporters should handle *non-urgent* peer support needs?

- What is the policy for urgent peer support needs? (In other words, what constitutes an urgent need? Is there a circumstance in which a peer supporter should not respond to an urgent need, but find someone else?)

See Appendix D for a sample set of time management rules.

By the way, let me offer some reassurance to leaders who are concerned that a peer support program will encourage employees to talk rather than work. Consider this—they talk anyway! The real question is whether their huddling will be destructive or constructive. With peer support, employees will do less destructive huddling because they know they will get to do a reasonable amount of constructive huddling. And leaders can use this time management policy to put parameters around the huddling and keep fine-tuning until they get it right.

## Create Confidentiality Ground Rules

An effective peer support program must have a confidentiality policy. Leadership must clearly specify when privacy will be honored and under what circumstances it can be compromised.

For example, can privacy be compromised if the peer supporter sincerely believes there is a clear and present danger? What about if the peer supporter sincerely believes that there might be a *future* danger to customers, the community, employees, etc.

What is the procedure if a peer supporter violates the confidentiality policy?

Appendix E offers a set of sample confidentiality rules.

The organization's legal representative should be involved with this policy.

## Designate Peer Support Meeting Spaces

It is helpful to designate places where peer support meetings can take place. You will also need to answer the following questions:

- What are the times these spaces will be available?

- How does a peer supporter reserve the space?

- Are peer supporters allowed to meet in non-designated places (e.g., a coffee shop?).

The organization's legal representative should be involved with this policy.

## Implement a Peer Support Alert System

This is the system that tells people in need of peer support who is on the peer support team and how to obtain peer support. This might involve a peer support email, text, or hotline that goes to a central dispatch. It may be providing a list of peer supporters and their contact information. It might also involve peer supporters wearing badges, armbands, pins, or other insignia that identifies them as peer supporters.

## Create Problem Escalation and Referral Procedure

There should be a clear system that peer supporters can use when they need to escalate or refer people. If escalation is necessary, who is next in the escalation chain? A peer support supervisor? A staff counselor? A workplace chaplain or coach?

It is also important to identify all resources available to the organization (e.g., outside counseling, financial counselors, mediators, etc.) This list will help when peer supporters need to refer a person to someone with specialized expertise.

## Organize a Support Structure for Peer Supporters

Create a support system that peer supporters can access when they are needing counsel about a person they are helping or about their own health. Determine who supervises the peer supporters (e.g., a chaplain, coach, staff psychologist, experienced peer supporter lead, etc.)

Be sure that peer support supervisors check in regularly (weekly or monthly) with peer supporters. Have quarterly meetings where peer supporters receive further training, encouragement, and where they can compare notes.

## Consider Having Employees Sign a Liability Waiver

I have included a sample boilerplate waiver in Appendix F. You will want to get your organization's legal representation involved.

I recommend that employees sign the waiver before launching the peer support program. This is better than having to figure this out in the middle of a crisis. Signing the waiver can be part of an information session explaining how the peer support program works. New hires can sign the waiver during their intake process, where they will presumably be informed about the peer support benefit.

## Communicate to All Employees

Use the designated communication channels discussed in Chapter Seven to inform all employees about the peer support programs. You'll want to include answers to the following questions: What is peer support? Why is peer support important? How to use peer support when it's needed.

You will already have introduced this concept when you recruit people. There is a sample communication template you can use for ideas in Appendix B.

## Formally Launch the Program

People generally need to know that the peer support program will become effective, starting on a specific date. It will likely take a while for people to begin to use it. A formal launch date will help avoid misunderstandings about whether it's okay to start using it.

## Share Success Stories

Sharing success stories will help you recruit more peer supporters and encourage employees to use peer support if they need it. These could be anonymous stories, but personal testimonies are even better. You can also take anonymous surveys about who is using peer support and how much they think it helps. Share these success stories via the channels you designated in Chapter Seven.

## Address High Risk, Low Use Conditions

You may have a situation where you think there is a high risk of emotional strain on employees, yet you are concerned that few people are using peer support when they need it. This can be a common scenario in law enforcement, for example.

In such situations, it is important to be patient and consistent. Keep reassuring people and giving testimonies—it takes time to break through cultures of toughness.

If this isn't working, a technique that can be very effective is to require everyone in the organization to sit with a professional (either an internal professional or external professional like a chaplain, coach, or counselor). Employees should not be pressured to say anything during the session if they don't want to. The only requirement is that they show up for ten minutes once or twice a year. This will make it safe for everyone, and some number of those who need to talk will talk.

# Questions for Reflection and Discussion

1. What do you think of the idea of peer support? Do you think it could be helpful? Does it make you nervous? Why?

2. Take a look at the "In session peer support techniques." Which of these do you think you could do well, and which do you think would challenge you?

3. Look through the list of "Principles to Follow." Do any of these principles surprise you? Do you agree or disagree with any of them? Why?

4. Do you think you would be a good peer supporter? Why or why not?

5. What do you think will be the greatest challenges to implementing peer support at your organization? Can you think of ways that these challenges can be overcome?

# Solution Three Section Summary

As we conclude this section, remember that the objective of these two chapters is to address complaining caused by pain and by a bad attitude. Both reasons for complaining are addressed by creating a culture of self-reflection and peer support.

Remember that self-reflection and peer support complement and balance each other. As people become more self-aware, they become more in touch with their internal motivations and their external behavior. Peer support can be a vital part of this process. And, of course, peer support can provide comfort to hurting people and hold people accountable who are struggling to overcome a bad attitude.

Self-reflection and peer support are the mechanisms that will facilitate the cultural change we are seeking. Individual employees will become healthier and happier, and relationships will become stronger and more satisfying.

This will be good for everyone!

CHAPTER THIRTEEN

# Next Steps

As we arrive at the last chapter, let me reiterate that we are talking about a process of cultural transformation. In other words, we're trying to create habits and values that are *naturally* practiced by *most* people in the organization.

Some organizations are already pretty good at solving problems, communicating with one another, and working out disagreements. For these organizations, the 'no complaining' process will help to refine their culture and become even better.

Other organizations are dealing with more cultural stress. Perhaps employee morale could be better. Perhaps there are segments of the organization that feel alienated from the rest. Perhaps there is mistrust between leadership and employees. If your organization is experiencing some of these challenges, the 'no complaining' process can help it heal and grow, though you'll need patience, commitment, consistency—and maybe some outside help. Here are some next steps that can help.

# Follow the Process

We've just spent many pages examining the details of the 'no complaining' process, so it's probably a good idea to remember the simplicity of the system. This is important because we want everyone in the organization to be able to follow the same simple way of thinking.

**Fundamentally, the process is: ALERT→APPLY (filter)→ACT**

**ALERT**—the Alert phase is where we notice that complaining is happening. That triggers the application of a filter where we determine the reason for the complaining.

**APPLY**—next we apply a filter by asking, "why is this complaining happening?" and determining which of the following options seems most likely:

- I am feeling helpless
- I am feeling frustrated by a problem
- I am in pain
- I have a bad attitude

**ACT**—depending upon the reason for the complaining, we take appropriate action:

- IF I am feeling helpless → THEN use Honoring Honesty to share my concerns with the appropriate people

- IF I am feeling frustrated by a problem → THEN employ the process of Problem Naming and Problem Solving

- IF I am in pain → THEN use Peer Support and Self-Awareness to pursue comfort, acceptance, and coping

- IF I have a bad attitude → THEN then use Peer Support and Self-Awareness to pursue growth and accountability

See Appendix A for a chart summarizing this process.

As you move into the appropriate actions, use this book as a reference. Turn to the appropriate section and let it guide you. Over time, this will become more natural for most people, and the organizational culture will change.

# Why Complaining Will Decrease

As more and more people in the organization follow the 'no complaining' process, complaining will diminish. As a reminder, I am speaking of unhealthy, destructive complaining, not constructive identification and resolution of concerns. But this unproductive complaining will diminish for one of the following reasons.

## *The Issue Will Be Resolved*

Whatever was causing the concern or problem is now resolved. This benefits the person who originally had the complaint, and it likely benefits others as well—maybe the entire organization.

## *The Person Will Be Able to Make Peace with the Concern*

The person with the complaint will understand why the situation is what it is and will be able to accept it. The person will at least feel like he has been heard, even though he might still disagree. And he'll be able to accept and cope with the condition.

## *Chronic Complainers Will Leave*

As more and more people engage complaining in constructive ways, even chronic complainers will begin to be transformed. This will be life-changing for habitually negative people. Sadly, there are always those who refuse even to try to change. Those people will likely leave the organization. They might leave voluntarily because their negativity is no longer indulged as it once was. Or, in some tragic cases, it will become clear to management that they have to ask the person to leave the organization.

It's really pretty simple. As an increasing number of people in the organization pursue the 'no complaining' system, unhealthy complaining will begin to go away for one of those reasons.

# The Importance of Including Everyone

In keeping with the theme of being as practical as possible, I want to point out some common mistakes I see organizations make. When it comes to the ideas found in a book like this, often only one (or a handful) of people in the organization embrace them. The problem is that cultural change is hard. It requires a critical mass of people in an organization to move together in the same direction. Cultural change is not something that can only be embraced by a few people. The more people included in the process, the more likely the organization will see real change.

When it comes to organizational cultural change, I see one of three general mistakes organizations make.

## Mistake 1—Relying on a Small Vanguard

Some organizations assign a small vanguard (e.g., a few people in the human resources department) to live out the cultural change ideas. The thinking is that this vanguard will learn deeply about the system, put the ideas into practice, and somehow their experience will rub off on the rest of the organization. The problem with this is that cultural change doesn't usually leak into the rest of the organization. Everyone is far too busy doing their jobs and just surviving among the noise and clutter that is organizational life.

Often this approach is pursued with the reasonable intention of "trying something out" before including the rest of the organization. Unfortunately, the limited scope of the effort never develops enough critical mass to create real change. Leadership therefore concludes that it is not effective, and the effort is abandoned—or at least left to slowly dry up.

## Mistake 2—Only Training Executives

Executives tend to receive most of the leadership training that organizations offer. This frequently includes topics such as those found in this book.

It is certainly important to train executives well because they generally have a disproportionate impact on the organization. Nevertheless, when trying to change or refine organizational culture, relevant training must get down deep into the bowels of the organization. It is a mistake to believe that training provided to an executive team will trickle down into the deepest crevices of the organization.

To create a 'no complaining' culture, *everyone* in the organization must agree to work towards the same goal. This means that *everyone* must be committed to noticing when real complaining is happening (and of course it will because this isn't a perfect process). Everyone must agree that when they notice complaining in any form—from themselves or others—they must name it, recognize it as a symptom of something that needs to be fixed, seek to understand what's at the root of it, and go to work to address the cause.

## Mistake 3—Leaving the Executives Out

Organizational culture training that is intended for the entire organization is by necessity going to be somewhat rudimentary. This is necessary because such training might be the first of its kind that many in the organization have received. Many executives have received advanced training in some form (e.g., business school, executive coaching or workshops, self-study, etc.). Therefore, executives are frequently looking for more advanced information and will be tempted to ignore a book like this due to its introductory nature.

The problem here is that for cultural change to happen, the executive team must buy-in and lead the way. Executives must at least have a familiarity with the principles and vocabulary found in this book. Remember, a significant part of creating a 'no complaining' organizational culture is teaching employees how to interact with executives, so executives need to know what to expect and be able to recognize and embrace the forms in which this communication comes to them from their followers.

## Use This Book as a Common Agreement

Because change in organizational culture requires a critical mass of people in the organization from executive to line level, this book can serve as a sort of an agreement that all can use to increase the likelihood that it will be followed. When everyone in the organization is trying to practice these principles, each person's effort will reinforce everyone else's effort.

When this is happening, momentum will build. Conversely, if everyone is following different approaches, using different vocabulary, and citing different sources, the effort will become watered down and will be less likely to gain traction.

A common agreement (such as the material in this book) can get everyone in the organization aligned and dramatically increase the likelihood of success.

## Consider Forming Discussion Groups

People learn by discussing and doing. Therefore, it can be a helpful reinforcement to organize groups that will meet periodically to discuss the contents of this book. These discussion groups are not the same as peer support. The purpose is to become familiar with the contents of the book, discuss the real-life application of its content, and share examples.

The discussion questions at the end of each chapter can guide conversation. Some chapters will take longer to go through than others, so participants should take their time. Participants can revisit chapters when necessary. You can certainly use these meetings to disseminate specifics to the program, such as designated communications channels, peer support policies, and so on.

I recommend that you have these groups meet once each week for the first three to six months of the 'no complaining' culture initiative. Limit weekly discussions to only 30 minutes or so. Encourage people to make these meetings a priority. Even people who feel they have mastered the material should attend these meetings faithfully. Others will benefit greatly from their insights.

There are several ways to consider organizing the groups. You could randomly assign people to groups. The advantage to this would be that participants would meet people on different teams and at varying levels in the organization. Or, you could have existing working teams meet for discussion. The advantage here is that this exercise can enhance teamwork.

## Plan Major Milestones

Like any project, creating a 'no complaining' organizational culture will probably not happen without a plan that guides people to action. Therefore, here is a practical list of major next steps to consider.

### *MILESTONE 1—Get Executive Commitment*

Nothing will happen without executive buy-in, and this must include the top executive. The first step, therefore, is to have the executive team familiarize themselves with the book's content. (I can do a one-hour executive overview for convenience). At this stage, it will also be critical to determine what self-awareness activity top executives will pursue since they must lead by example. This might be a 360-degree review, some executive coaching, or even a self-browse through this book where they highlight some personal revelations.

## *MILESTONE 2—Create an Implementation Timeline*

Once you have executive buy-in, you'll need to create an implementation timeline. For each milestone, you'll want to assign an estimated project duration, start and completion dates, and project owners. I have put a table in Appendix G that you can use.

## *MILESTONE 3—Identify Communication Channels*

Refer to Chapter Seven and the discussion of communications channels that will be used for communication about cultural initiatives, leadership updates, employee feedback, and problem solving.

## *MILESTONE 4—Begin Executive Communications*

Cultural change involves every person in the organization, but it must be led from the top. Executives should begin communications that explain why a 'no complaining' culture will benefit everyone in the organization (refer to Appendix B for a sample e-mail/speech). These executive communications should happen at least weekly, leading up to the launch of the 'no complaining' culture initiative.

## *MILESTONE 5—Implement Peer Support*

Refer to Chapter Twelve for details on how to implement the peer support structure. There is some lead time required for recruiting and training peer supporters, getting legal documents and peer support policies finalized, designating space for peer support, and planning alert systems, referral resources, and escalation procedures. You'll want to allow time to complete these tasks.

## *MILESTONE 6—Teach the Book's Content*

Figure out how you will teach the content to everyone in the organization. To work out the kinks, you might start with a certain workgroup or department. Formal peer supporters will have additional training tacked on.

## *MILESTONE 7—Do an Official Launch*

If the organization is large and it has taken some time to get everyone through the 'no complaining' culture training, it will probably be helpful to have an official launch date for the entire effort. This will help set everyone's expectations about when they can expect fellow employees to utilize and respond to the techniques discussed in this book. (This may be the same launch date as the peer support launch date I mentioned in Chapter Twelve, but it doesn't have to be.)

## *MILESTONE 8—Follow Up Assessments*

To maintain cultural transformation momentum and to refine the approach, it will be necessary to do follow up assessments. That might include anonymous surveys or interviewing a sampling of employees about how the 'no complaining' culture effort is going. Ask employees if they have implemented anything in the book, what seems to be working well, and what needs some improvement. This information can be shared with the organization in regular progress updates. I recommend that the first few follow up assessments be conducted quarterly. Frequency after that will depend upon progress.

# Conclusion

The creation of a 'no complaining' organizational culture will involve some work. If you'd like help, my organization, Remedium Solutions, can assist with certain parts of the implementation or manage the entire process.

Keep in mind that in highly stressed organizations, you may first need to do some disarming before employees will be willing to embrace an organizational culture initiative. Here again, Remedium Solutions can help. Our People Systems Diagnostics and Optimization process can identify the most pressing points of anxiety in the organization. We can then coach leadership about how to acknowledge those concerns and begin an honest dialogue about them.

Think of this process as setting out on a journey. It will take time, but it will pay dividends. The reduction in complaining is only the beginning. It will be accompanied by an increase in productivity, creativity, innovation, problem-solving, employee health, morale, retention, engagement, and other positive things that will advance the mission of your organization.

So, take the first step towards the creation of a 'no complaining' organizational culture. It will be good for everyone!

# Questions for Reflection and Discussion

1. Do you believe the ALERT→APPLY (filter)→ACT system can reduce complaining? Why or why not?

2. Why is it important to include everyone in creating a 'no complaining' organizational culture? What mistakes do some organizations make when pursuing cultural change initiatives?

3. In pursuing a 'no complaining' organizational culture, why is it important to have a common agreement? How can this book serve as a common agreement?

4. If complaining diminishes as a result of real organizational transformation, what other benefits do you think the employees, leaders, and the organization as a whole will experience? Can you think of people outside of the organization who will be positively affected? Give some examples.

# The 'No Complaining' Process

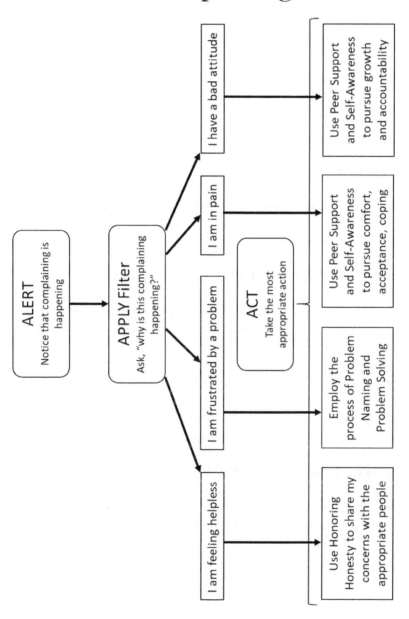

APPENDIX B

# Sample Speech/Email

**Here are general some points to include in executive communications:**

- We care about our employees, and it is important to us that our employees feel like they matter.
- We want our employees to be healthy and happy at work and in their personal lives.
- We want to create (reinforce) a healthy organizational culture that helps reduce frustration and increase satisfaction.
- To do this, starting on [date], we will begin a journey together to implement a program that will help us create lasting change.
- If we are all committed to make this work, we can create an environment that everyone feels good about.

**Here are some points to make about the program:**

- The program we'll use is based upon a book called *How to Create a 'No Complaining' Organizational Culture (...and Why It Will Be Good for Everyone)*.
- Let me assure you that we are not trying to silence people.
- Rather, we will learn together how to use complaining (something we all do at times) as a signal that alerts us to a problem that needs to be addressed.
- And we will learn to address those problems in constructive ways that will benefit everyone in the organization.
- On this journey, we'll all learn how to communicate better—peer to peer, leader to follower, and follower to leader.
- We'll learn to solve problems together better.
- We'll learn how to help one another grow as people.
- And we'll learn how to support each other with some of the challenges life gives us.

**Here are some points to make about peer support:**

- One of the ways we will grow and support one another is through a peer support program
- We will train some of our fellow employees to be peer supporters who are available to help us when we need it.
- Being a peer supporter is a meaningful way to encourage others when they face challenges in the office or other areas of their lives.
- If you are willing to consider becoming a peer supporter, please come to the peer support information session on [date].

APPENDIX C

# Peer Supporter Application

Your name:

Your email:

Your phone number:

**Thank you for your interest in helping your fellow employees. Your answers to the questions below will help us as we form the peer support team.**

1. Why do you want to be a peer supporter?

2. Can you commit to being a peer supporter for one year (barring any unforeseen problems)?

3. Are you willing to participate in the training and other activities required of peer supporters?

4. Are you *currently* dealing with any *major* emotional or life challenges?

5. Do you have any questions about peer support? (please write them here)

APPENDIX D

# Time Management Parameters

Peer supporters should use their best efforts to conduct peer support according to the following guidelines:

- Peer supporters are expected to fulfill their normal work responsibilities. To minimize misunderstandings, peer supporters should work closely with their supervisors to adjust their workload in a way that allows them to fulfill their peer support responsibilities and meet their supervisor's expectations.

- Peer supporters may dedicate up to _____ minutes (or hours) per week to supporting peers during working hours. The peer supporter's work supervisor must approve additional peer support time.

- Peer support training activities do not count toward this limit.

- Peer support conducted during lunch hours or outside of the involved employees' normal working hours does not count toward this limit.

- Emergency peer support does not count toward this limit.

- Employees should make best efforts for non-emergency peer support to occur during the following time windows:

    [designate preferred time windows here]

APPENDIX E

# Confidentiality Policy

**(Please note that this is just a sample. It is not a legal document. Any legal documents must be approved by your organization's legal representation)**

Peer supporters are expected to keep confidential any information shared with them by someone seeking peer support, *except* under one or more of the following conditions:

- When sharing confidential information is clearly in the best interest of the person receiving peer support (e.g., telling a paramedic about a medication the person is taking, if that person is unconscious)

- When there is a clear and present threat to the person receiving peer support or to other people (e.g., a threat of suicide or revenge)

- Under legal order

Possible consequences for breaking this policy include dismissal from the peer support program, termination of employment, or legal proceedings.

APPENDIX F

# Sample Liability Waiver

**(Please note that this is just a sample. It is not a legal document. Any legal documents must be approved by your organization's legal representation)**

I understand that the peer supporter(s) I am seeing is providing a free service to me in good faith, in a manner that is commensurate with [organization name's] training and best practices, with the intention of helping me. I release [organization name] and its peer supporters from liability for any harm or perceived harm I incur from the services I am receiving through the peer support program.

I understand that [organization name] offers peer support services to all people, irrespective of gender, religion, ethnicity, personal preferences, or lifestyle. I understand that if I decide to seek services from another peer supporter or a professional helper, [organization name] will attempt to connect me with one.

I understand that [organization name] or the peer supporter I am seeing does NOT recommend that I discontinue any medications or medical treatment without the advice and consent of the doctor that prescribed the medication or treatment.

I understand that there is no fee for the peer support services I receive from [organization name's] peer supporters, nor is there an expectation that I will make a donation to any peer supporter. There may, however, be expenses associated with other services I decide to pursue outside of the peer support structure.

I understand that any information I share with [organization name] peer supporters will be kept with discretion. [Organization name] peer supporters working with me will only share information with appropriate parties when it is clearly in my best interest, when there is a clear and present threat to me or other people, or under legal order.

APPENDIX G

# Major Milestones

| MILESTONE | START DATE | COMPLETION DATE | PROJECT OWNER |
|---|---|---|---|
| Get Executive Commitment | | | |
| Create an Implementation Timeline | | | |
| Identify Communication Channels | | | |
| Begin Executive Communications | | | |
| Implement Peer Support | | | |
| Teach the Book's Content | | | |
| Do an Official Launch | | | |
| Follow Up Assessments | | | |

# About the Author

Scott Maurer is Founder and President of Remedium Solutions, LLC, a firm that helps organizations make positive work culture a competitive advantage. Scott designed the Remedium People Systems Diagnostics and Optimization process to help organizations discover and heal dysfunction and maximize the way their people work together. This results in decreased costs, increased profitability, and more effective mission achievement.

Scott brings 30 years of wide-ranging experiences that have provided him with the skills needed to help organizations heal and thrive. This includes 15 years of business experience (from entry to executive level), and 15 years leading churches as a head pastor while running a non-profit counseling and mental health training organization. He has over 10,000 hours of counseling and coaching experience and a doctorate focusing on secular leadership, followership, team theory, emotional intelligence, conflict resolution, change management, and other aspects of individual and group psychology.

Though Scott's work with Remedium Solutions is non-religious in approach, it does draw on his knowledge of people and relationship system dynamics from his counseling, church leadership, and business experience. Businesses and churches have some similarities and some differences. Each has a *transactional dynamic* consisting of the tasks and goals that individuals and teams must accomplish to achieve the organization's mission. Each also has a *family dynamic* consisting of the interpersonal relationships among the people. In a church, the family dynamic is the main thing. But if the transactional elements are overlooked, the church will struggle to organize volunteers, care for the building, or manage its finances. In a business, the transactional dynamic is the main thing. But if the family dynamic is overlooked in a business, the organization becomes like an engine with no oil. Eventually, it breaks down. That is why a former pastor and counselor with business experience is the ideal person to help organizations address their family dynamics so they can keep most of their focus on the transactional elements of their mission.

To learn more about Remedium Solutions, please see our website at **www.remediumsolutions.com**.

You can contact Scott at **scott@remediumsolutions.com**.

Made in the USA
Middletown, DE
14 February 2020